BRITISH COLUMBIA–YUKON

STERNWHEEL DAYS

BY ART DOWNS

The Nasutlin trapped in the ice above Mayo, Yukon, in the fall of 1919. Ice was a serious hazard to navigation on the Yukon River and its tributaries in both fall and spring and crushed many sternwheelers.

CONTENTS

PHOTO CAPTIONS

THESE PAGES: The *Inlander* churns past Ringbolt Island in Kitselas Canyon on the Skeena River in 1911. It wasn't unusual for a sternwheeler to spend six or more hours fighting up a canyon or rapids, then on the down-stream trip shooting through in minutes at speeds up to 30 miles an hour.

PAGES 4-5: Entries from Captain O. F. Browne's log book for the opening of the 1906 navigation season on the Upper Fraser River. The *Charlotte* was launched at Quesnel in 1896.

May. 15th 1906.

Str Charlotte.

Trial Trip to Cotton wood Canyon
April 30th. Returned at 7.15 and arrived Quesnell
at 8.30. everything all. O.K.

Then Started on Regular Trips May 1st
Started at 9.30. to ferry horses to Bushea's ldg
to Bushea. 10 Stopped at Geo. Adam's wood yard
and also at Chinese wood yard. tried to land
down stream but the boat would not handle
so proceeded on down River. Stopped at Twann's
ldg. to Twanns and arr. at Soda Creek. about
3. P.m. all. O.K.

May 2nd/06

lv. Soda Creek for Quesnell at 4.05 a m
Passed Makin Creek at 5.10 a. m. Stopped to take
on a pig at Chinaman's Ranch but Pig Run away
so we proceeded without pig lost 10 minute.
Stopped at Twanns ldg took on some horses at
8. am Crossed over to Ind. Res. put off horses +
Started for Websters Cattle Carroll took on 4 head
of beef Cattle for Quesnell meat market. Started
again about 9 a.m. Stopped at Chinese lower
wood yard for Mr Fraser to measure some wood
after measuring. Started and picked up a mowing
Mach- which was left last fall by wrecking crew
then proceeded up River put off Wm Schippas at
Wale's ldg.

May 6th /06

Left Soda Creek at 3.48. a.m. Passed Mackin
Creek 4.40. Chinese Ranch 5.30 took on
Some Potatoes & escaped pig. then left for
up River Passed ah Sings Ranch. 6.47 arr
Twanns ldg 7.30 left 7.35. arr Anders P.O. 7.50 left
8.05. Passed Castle Rock. 9.45. Aus Ranch 10.40
3 hr. P. 11.14 adams W.P. 12.05 9 mile Claim 12.55
    Arr Quesnell. 2.15. all. O.K.

May 8th /06

Left Quesnell 11 a.m. arr Wood yd. 12.00
took on wood then left for down River
at 1.20. P.m. Passed Castle Rock 2.50 P.m.
    arr Soda Creek ferry ldg 4. oclock took on
about 7.1/2 Tons of hay for Soda Creek. left
fery ldg about 7. P.m + tied up about 7.40.
    all O.K. boat visited by School Children

May 9th

Left Soda Creek for Quesnell & way ldgs
at 3.52. Passed Mackin Creek. 4.50. Chinese R.
5.37. ah Sing R. 6.35. stopped at Mc Innis ldg 7.01
put off lady & Children left 7.12. Spark Catcher
stopped up run slow to Twanns ldg stop at Twann
7.30 left 7.58. Anders P.O. 8. a.m. put mail off
and waited Spark Catcher was cleaned out
left 8.13. Passed Castle Rock 9.50. Aus R. ldg 10.35
pick up two Inds left 10.40. 3 hr. Point 11.18. 9 mile
Claim 12.57. arr Quesnell 2.15. tied up all OK

International under full steam on Kootenay Lake.

FOREWORD

The events narrated in this book are not fiction. Each happened to a paddlewheeler, its crew or its passengers on the major lakes and rivers plus coastal waterways of British Columbia and the Yukon. The era opened in March 1836 when the Hudson's Bay Company's *Beaver* arrived on the Pacific Coast and closed in April 1957 when the venerable *Moyie* was retired from service on Kootenay Lake. The men who manned the vessels are largely gone, over 300 boats as well, their bones scattered throughout the multi-thousand-square-mile area of British Columbia and the Yukon.

In B.C. only one sternwheeler has been fully preserved, the *Moyie* at Kaslo on Kootenay Lake. Here she hosts thousands of visitors every year. At Penticton, the *Sicamous* has been hauled ashore but has not been preserved. At New Westminster the *Sampson V* has survived and is open to the public but she was never a commercial craft. Her career was as a Federal Government work boat helping keep the Fraser River clear of snags and other debris.

In the Yukon, of some 250 vessels, two have survived. They are the *Klondike* at Whitehorse and the *Keno* at Dawson City, both now protected and maintained as National Historic Sites and open to the public. Fortunately, the record that the vessels wrote on rivers, lakes and ocean has been compiled.

The dean of paddlewheel historians is Norman Hacking, author and for many years marine editor of the *Vancouver Province*. His series of articles on the Lower Fraser River and the Upper Columbia and Kootenay Rivers in the *B.C. Historical Quarterly* are outstanding and have been used as source material by dozens of writers. Another excellent article for the same publication was written by the late Willis J. West and captured the flavor of sternwheel days on the Upper Fraser River in Cariboo and Central B.C. The Skeena River had its chronicler in that grand old pioneer, Wiggs O'Neill of Smithers. Wiggs, like Willis West, took part in the sternwheel saga and wrote from personal experience.

For the Okanagan, the Annual Reports of the Okanagan Historical Society are a treasure of information and certainly the most ambitious and comprehensive district biography compiled by a regional B.C. Historical Society. Considerable data on the Kamloops-Shuswap region has been gathered by the Kamloops Museum Association and is a fine reference. For the Kootenay-Arrow Lakes area Captain J. Fitzsimmons and E. L. Affleck have excellent material, with Mr. Affleck in particular compiling a comprehensive manuscript. For the Atlin and Bennett Lakes region of northern B.C., and the Yukon River, W. D. MacBride tracked the career of over 200 sternwheelers. And since the Klondike stampede has been probably the best chronicled gold rush in history with over 100 books written by participants, there are scores of personal accounts of the sternwheelers that plied the waters and headwaters of the Yukon.

The biggest single cargo of information, however, is the Provincial Archives at Victoria. Here in row after row, shelf after shelf, is filed just about every copy of every newspaper ever published in B.C. and Yukon. These papers—many with fading ink and greying pages that reflect their age of a century or more—contain eye-witness accounts, first-hand reports and a host of other data on vessels and their crews. The *Victoria Colonist* is a particular treasure. It is the only paper in B.C. that has been continuously published since the rousing days of the 1858 Fraser River gold rush.

The record that paddlewheelers and their crews left ranges from comic to tragic, from merely impossible to incredible. This book is not intended to be a concise history of these events. It endeavours instead to present a broad picture of the vessels and their crews and the contribution both made in the transformation of a frontier to the land we know today.

PHOTO CREDITS

The author thanks the following government agencies, companies, historical societies and individuals: B.C. Provincial Archives, C.P.R., Cominco, Glenbow Foundation, Geological Survey of Canada, Government of Alberta, H.B.C., Historical Society of Alaska, Kamloops Museum Assn., Kelowna Historical Society, Kootenay Lake Historical Society, Kootenay Museum Assn., Libby Pioneer Society, National Film Board, National Museum of Canada, Notman Photographic Archives, Public Archives of Canada, Quesnel Historical Society, Vancouver City Archives, Vancouver Public Library, University of Alaska, Whitehorse Star, White Pass and Yukon Railway and Yukon Dept. of Travel and Information.

Among individuals who responded or deserve credit as the original photographer are E. Anderson, F. Button, D. Clemson, J. G. Craft, Mrs. Dunne, Eric Erickson, Mrs. R. Horsey, Mrs. E. Louie, Jim McClelland, W. F. Montgomery, Eric Sismey, J. Simonson, J. E. Parker, W. Wilson, and W. W. Wrathall. The latter was a pioneer Skeena River photographer whose sternwheel pictures rank among the best. Many other early photographers also took excellent photos, but their names have unfortunately been lost with the passage of the years.

Copyright © 1972-1992 Art Downs

CANADIAN CATALOGUING IN PUBLICATION DATA

Downs, Art, 1924-
    B.C.-Yukon sternwheel days

    First ed. has title: Paddlewheels on the Frontier.
    Includes index.
    ISBN 0-919214-63-0
    1. Paddle steamers — British Columbia —
History. 2. Paddle steamers — Yukon Territory —
History. I. Title. II. Title: Paddlewheels
on the frontier.
VM627.B7D69 1992   386'.22436   C92-091101-3

HERITAGE HOUSE PUBLISHING COMPANY LTD.
Box 1228, Station A
Surrey, B.C. V3S 2B3

Printed in Canada

". . . from the misty rivers comes call of trusty friend,
For foaming bows of river boat are 'coming 'round the bend'."

STERNWHEEL SAGA

There's a river boat a-wooding up beside a muddy bank,
Safety valves a-screaming; now they're hauling in the plank
And the great wheel starts a-churning,—she's a-shaping Destiny,
A-heading up the river through an empire yet to be.

She's a-heading up the river; the labored breath of steam
Echoes from bench and woodland along the winding stream,
And anxious hearts are waiting where lonely cabins stand,—
Where wood-smoke marks outposts of men across a lonely land.

Now she's whistling for a landing,—she's a-comin 'round the bend,
She's a life-line in the wilderness,—and pioneers true friend,
And she shares the conquest of the land with matron, man and maid,
Who fight with sickle, axe and plow, stout-hearted, unafraid!

From NORTHLAND TRAILS by S. C. ELLS

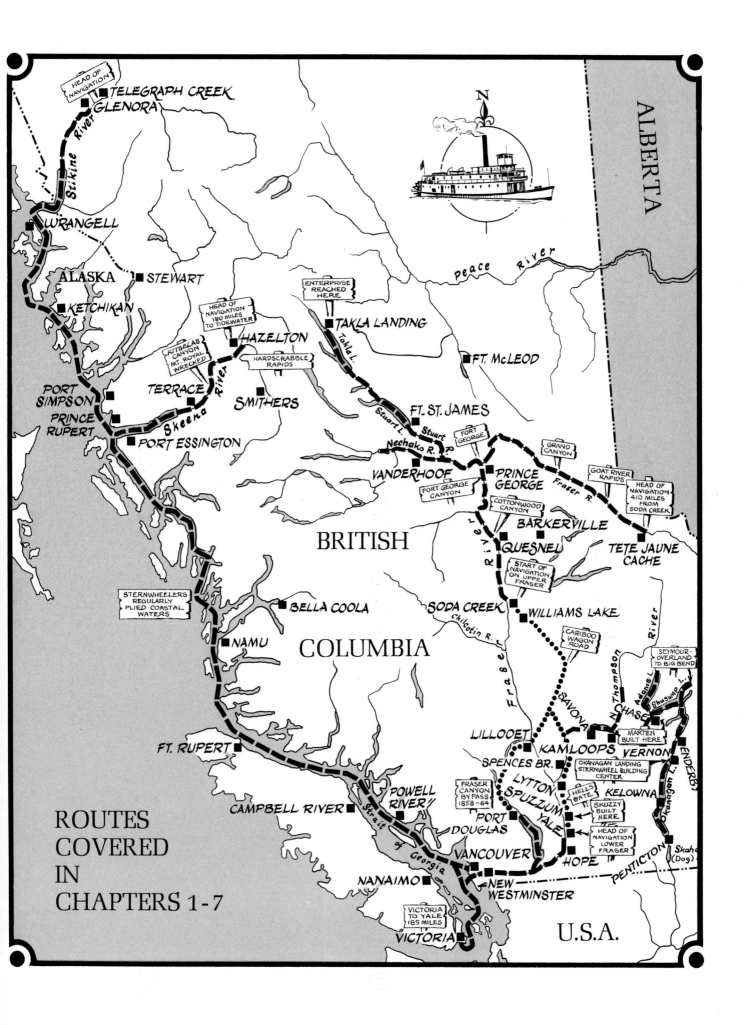

HEAD OF NAVIGATION

TELEGRAPH CREEK
GLENORA

Stikine River

WRANGELL

ALASKA STEWART

KETCHIKAN

PORT SIMPSON

PRINCE RUPERT

PORT ESSINGTON

Skeena River

KITSELAS CANYON MT. ROYAL WRECKED

HEAD OF NAVIGATION 180 MILES TO TIDEWATER

HAZELTON

TERRACE

SMITHERS

HARDSCRABBLE RAPIDS

ENTERPRISE REACHED HERE

TAKLA LANDING

Takla L.

FT. McLEOD

Peace River

ALBERTA

N

Stuart L.

Stuart

FT. ST. JAMES

Nechako R.

FORT GEORGE

VANDERHOOF

FORT GEORGE CANYON

PRINCE GEORGE

Fraser R.

GRAND CANYON

GOAT RIVER RAPIDS

HEAD OF NAVIGATION 410 MILES FROM SODA CREEK

COTTONWOOD CANYON

BARKERVILLE

QUESNEL

TETE JAUNE CACHE

BRITISH

COLUMBIA

BELLA COOLA

STERNWHEELERS REGULARLY PLIED COASTAL WATERS

NAMU

SODA CREEK

Chilcotin R.

START OF NAVIGATION ON UPPER FRASER

WILLIAMS LAKE

River

Fraser River

CARIBOO WAGON ROAD

Thompson River

Adams L.

Shuswap L.

SEYMOUR-OVERLAND TO BIG BEND

SAVONA

CHASE

N. Thompson

MARTEN BUILT HERE

VERNON

LILLOOET

KAMLOOPS

ENDERBY

FT. RUPERT

POWELL RIVER

Strait of Georgia

CAMPBELL RIVER

SPENCES BR.

OKANAGAN LANDING STERNWHEEL BUILDING CENTER

LYTTON

SPUZZUM

YALE

HELLS GATE

SKUZZY BUILT HERE

KELOWNA

Okanagan L.

FRASER CANYON BY PASS 1858-64

PORT DOUGLAS

HEAD OF NAVIGATION LOWER FRASER

VANCOUVER

HOPE

PENTICTON

Skaha (Dog)

NANAIMO

NEW WESTMINSTER

ROUTES COVERED IN CHAPTERS 1-7

VICTORIA TO YALE 185 MILES

VICTORIA

U.S.A.

CHAPTER ONE

The Vessels

Sternwheel steamers were remarkable craft. In a century of service on the lakes, rivers and coastal waters of British Columbia and the Yukon they were splintered by boiler explosions, gutted by fires, crushed by ice, swamped by gales and disemboweled by rapids, yet they served wherever they were needed and for as long as they were required. Well over 300 plied the waterways of this 572,000-square-mile area, some blowing or burning up almost on their maiden voyage, others sailing so long they became one of the family to pioneer settlers.

Although the bluff-bowed vessels are popularly associated with the Mississippi River, they were used more extensively in B.C. than in any other area of North America. Their shrill whistles reverberated over lakes that included Arrow, Adams, Atlin, Columbia, Fraser, Kamloops, Kootenay, Okanagan, Shuswap, Stuart, Takla, Tagish, Thompson, Trembleur, Trout, and Windermere. Their paddlewheels churned a rainbow of foam on rivers such as Columbia, Fraser, Kootenay, Nechako, Nass, Okanagan, Peace, Skeena, Stuart, Spallumcheen, Stikine, and Thompson. Their wakes rippled coastal gulfs and straits from Juan de Fuca in the south to Hecate and beyond in the north. During the Klondike rush, for instance, they churned northward from Victoria to the Gulf of Alaska, beat through the storm-lashed Bering Sea, then up Yukon River to Whitehorse, a hazardous voyage covering some 4,500 miles. But this type of challenge was nothing exceptional for sternwheelers. Their job, as one veteran skipper observed, was to do the impossible—and do it profitably.

Their success was due to a combination of factors, one of which was a flat bottom which enabled them to bob on the water like a duck. Another was that their wooden construction made them remarkably buoyant and fairly easy to repair. On Upper Fraser River the *B.X.* once gouged a hole

Sternwheelers evolved into perfect craft for frontier waterways. Tough, powerful, and easy to build, they could carry 100 or more tons of freight plus passengers in water little deeper than required by a canoe, yet regularly challenged rapids and canyons where canoes needed portaging. The Port Simpson, *shown on Skeena River about 1909, was typical of the breed.*

11

in her keel sixty feet long by three feet wide. She reached shore before sinking and a few weeks later was back in service.

Another asset was that their paddlewheel needed water only inches deep to supply its powerful thrust. On Thompson River the *Kamloops* worked in eight inches, the *Spallumcheen* could get by in six, while on Columbia River the *Duchess* sailed so close to the bottom that gravel ridged by spawning salmon was an obstacle. Because of this shallow draft, there is a story that one passenger who fell overboard raised a cloud of dust. Actually, the tale could be true. With a block and tackle device called a "grasshopper" rigged on the bow, vessels could hoist themselves over bars and shoals, and anyone then falling overboard would land with a thud rather than a splash.

Another story involves the captain of a sternwheeler stranded at the upper reaches of the Fraser by low water. As usually happens in Interior B.C., autumn rains caused the river to rise but not enough to cover the bar causing the

trouble. The skipper curbed his impatience for a couple of days then could wait no longer. "Okay, boys, let's hit it. The sand's wet. She'll go over."

Sternwheelers were as distinctly North American as the Pony Express and North West Mounted Police. They appeared originally on the Mississippi River about 1817, came west via the tip of South America during the 1849 California gold rush, north to the Columbia, then north again to Fraser River in 1858.

First vessels on the Fraser in 1858 were sidewheelers. They had two paddlewheels, one on each side about amidships, but soon proved unsatisfactory. They required a wharf, thus docking was a problem; they were hard to manage in narrow channels; and their exposed paddlewheels were easily jammed by debris and damaged by riverbanks.

A sternwheeler, by contrast, had a single paddlewheel at the stern. A wharf was therefore unnecessary, the bow was simply nosed ashore while the stern with its motive power remained in deep water. They were also easier to control in

narrow waterways and the hull acted as a shield for the paddlewheel. In B.C., sternwheelers quickly proved superior to sidewheelers and were used almost exclusively, although miners who were accustomed to sidewheelers thought sternwheelers odd.

"A queer-looking steamer, having the paddle wheels, minus boxes, in the stern," wrote one traveller, who soon learned the advantages of having one paddlewheel astern instead of two jutting from the sides. On a trip up Harrison River he noted: "The last part of the river was very narrow and we ran into the sides several times; once a tree caught some boxes of bacon and turned them over on the deck, smashing one of the number." Had the vessel been a sidewheeler, the river bank and overhanging trees would have also smashed her paddlewheels.

Sternwheelers varied in design from a packing crate to graceful queens sparkling with white paint and polished copper, and came in all shapes, sizes, and furnishings. "She is not at all a harbor of comfort," complained one passenger after travelling up the Fraser on a gold-rush vessel. Another passenger wrote angrily to the *Victoria Standard* that on Stikine River the *Hope* charged $25 for passage "and sleep in one's own blankets, cook for self, pay $1 for inferior grub, and occasionally cut wood, etc. . . ."

Besides cutting wood, passengers were called upon to help load the wood, or fight a fire on board, or surrender their blankets to plug a hole in the hull, or even jump into the cold water and help free the vessel from sand or gravel bar. During the Cariboo gold rush a miner who boarded a sternwheeler at New Westminster for Yale recorded that one passenger had a "bell thrust into his hand, and he was instructed to ring the bell and bawl at the top of his voice the departure of the boat; this he did to perfection, being a powerful man with strong lungs. The work lasted half an hour and he was given $2.50 for his pains."

Passengers were also at times victims of over optimism when owners pronounced the merits of their vessels. On the Lower Fraser River when the *Gem* was launched she was stated to be "the most complete little craft the province has produced." In 1887 English author Morley Roberts took passage on the "complete little craft" and mentioned his experiences in his book *The Western Avernus*: "Next afternoon the *Gem* steamer came downstream. Poor little wretched steamer to be so mis-called: *Coal Scuttle* or *Hog-Pen* would have made good names for her. The Captain and one more made up the crew—two all told. The captain usually steered, and the other man engineered and fired up, and one or the other would rush out on landing to hitch a rope round the stump; and when wood ran low they would run her ashore near a pile, the noble skipper getting out to throw half a cord on deck. Then they had to take it aft before they could back her off. So we made slow progress, even with the current of the noble river under us, especially as every little while we stopped to take a few squealing pigs on board or some sacks of potatoes."

The H.B.C. sidewheel steamer Beaver, pioneer of pioneers, off Victoria about 1870. The first steam-powered vessel on the entire Pacific Coast, she arrived in 1836 and was active until July 26, 1888 when she went aground at the entrance to Vancouver harbor.

On gold-rush era sternwheelers passenger accommodation was often as bare as a barracks, but later became plush and refined. Upper photo shows the ladies' lounge on the R. P. Rithet; center and lower the interior of the Slocan, on Slocan Lake, and Bonnington on the Arrow Lakes.

But as frontier days waned, meals and accommodation became so lavish that old-timers still recall them with sighs of appreciation. The *B.X.*, launched at Soda Creek in 1910 for service on Upper Fraser River, had steam-heated staterooms with red velvet carpeting, thick mattresses and expensive linen. Her dishes and crockery were especially made in England and she even had a bridal chamber with a $150 silk eiderdown. On many vessels meals were served in sparkling dining rooms complete with white tablecloths and silver finger bowls. But regardless whether the vessels were lavish or spartan, all had a common purpose—help open a frontier land.

Basically, sternwheelers were similar in design: good length and width (about 125′ x 30′ for the average vessel), with a somewhat blunt bow, and flat bottom without external keel. Because of their length and lack of outside keel, they sagged at bow and stern, so that iron braces called "hog-chains" or "hog-rods" were required to strengthen their hull. Although the method of strengthening varied from vessel to vessel, the principle was constant. Stubbed into the center keelson was a mast-like upright called a "kingpost" which towered above the top deck. Some vessels had one kingpost, others two, joined to bow and stern by the hog-chains. On either side of the kingposts were additional uprights called "hogposts," stubbed into another set of keelsons and also joined to bow and stern. Turnbuckles on the hog-chains provided adjustment to take up slack if bow or stern sagged, or release tension if the vessel became swaybacked. The idea was to keep the hull completely flat. As a mark of importance, kingposts were frequently decorated with brass or gold-painted balls, but hogposts carried no decorations.

The average sternwheeler had three decks. On the main deck were boiler, fire box, engine room, cargo space, and usually kitchen. The boiler was as far forward as possible to provide maximum draft for the fire, with steam piped aft to two, single-cylinder engines. Long connecting rods joined engines to the sternwheel, which extended across the width of vessel. The rudders—three to four—were mounted ahead of the sternwheel, with some vessels having two additional small rudders behind the sternwheel.

Usually between the main deck and the hull were watertight compartments appropriately christened "snag rooms." With one, two, or even more of these compartments punctured, the vessel generally could reach shore. Sternwheelers operating in coastal waters made additional use of these compartments by storing in them fresh water for the boiler.

Above the main deck was the cabin deck, known by various other names which included hurricane, saloon and promenade. On it were passenger cabins, dining room, and a saloon or observation lounge at bow or stern or both. Above the cabin deck was the upper, or texas deck, usually reserved for officers' quarters with the pilothouse at the forward part or even on top to ensure an unobstructed view.

Number of crew varied, with 12 to 17 average for river vessels but 25 or more on larger steamers such as the *Bonnington* on Arrow Lakes. As with ocean-going vessels, the captain was in complete charge and on rivers especially, his skill decided if the trip ended in success or disaster. There were no charts, and since B.C.'s mountain-fed waterways can rise five, ten, or more feet a day, he had to be constantly alert. Every change in water level meant new

dangers: familiar channels plugged, new bars created, spear-pointed snags stranded just below the surface, rapids changed in form and velocity. All these things he had to recognize by reading the surface, as well as remembering permanent hazards on 200, 300, or even 400 miles of ever dangerous river.

But even the most expert skipper couldn't avoid all perils, especially during low water. For this reason another crew member, the carpenter, was frequently busy.

Jim Williams, who worked on Upper Fraser River sternwheelers between Quesnel and Tete Jaune Cache, recalled that on one trip through seven-mile-long Giscome Rapids the *Quesnel* had 15 holes punched in her hull. These holes were repaired with a "soft patch," usually a wad of oakum slapped on the hole and held in place by a post wedged against the deck. If there was no oakum, sacks of flour or anything soft was substituted. Many a side of bacon became a temporary hull patch rather than a companion for breakfast eggs.

Besides the carpenter, others in the deck crew were the

Piloting a sternwheeler on any river in B.C.-Yukon was hazardous, with the Fraser, Stikine, Kootenay, Columbia, and Skeena in particular slashed by rapids and canyons. To skippers, however, these hazards were just a normal part of the day's work. George V. Copley, who in 1910 was a member of a survey party travelling up the Nechako River on the Chilco, left the following account of her battle to ascend Isle-de-Pierre Rapids in the photo above:

"We finally came to our first difficulty, Isle-de-Pierre Rapids,

mate and deckhands, the latter varying from four to more. Their main duty was handling freight. Since vessels generally sailed at dawn, loading was done at night, and stowing aboard 100 or more tons of freight with hand carts often meant long hours. After putting in an 18-hour shift, one new deckhand on a Kootenay Lake sternwheeler wearily turned to a companion and asked, "When do we get to sleep on this job?"

"Don't know," replied the other. "I only joined the boat three days ago."

The steward's department varied according to the number of passengers but included a steward, cook, and one or more waiters and galley staff. Also aboard were a purser, a freight clerk, and before prohibition, often a bartender. In the engine room were two engineers and two firemen, plus two coal passers on large sternwheelers such as the C.P.R.'s *Sicamous*. Unlike the latter vessel, however, most sternwheelers burned wood.

A sternwheeler under full steam on lake or river was a colorful spectacle still remembered with nostalgia by those who saw them. The late Wiggs O'Neill, Bulkley Valley pioneer, historian, and part owner of the *Inlander*, last paddlewheeler on Skeena River, wrote the following account: "In sight and sound a sternwheeler chugging upriver has been likened to a steam locomotive. Like a locomotive most sternwheelers used non-condensing engines; that is, the steam, instead of being put through condensers and used again, is discharged right into the smoke stack. This serves the purpose of giving the fire forced draft, making it possible to burn any kind of wood, wet or dry.

"This was the reason, too, that a sternwheeler bucking current could be heard for miles since the steam exhausted into the stack with a roar. The sound was similar to a steam locomotive leaving a station, except that locomotives used a valve that allowed steam to escape all at once, producing the characteristic puff—puff—puff. A sternwheeler used a slide valve that allowed the steam to escape more gradually, making a long screeching sound, something like phew—

one-quarter-mile long and too steep for the steamer to navigate. All hands off to drag a one-inch steel cable to the head of the rapids, to be made fast to a sizeable spruce tree.

"All went well until the steamer was about one-half way up the rapids, then without warning the spruce tree came out, roots and all. The steamer slewed around crosswise to the stream and down we went, bumpty bump over the rocks. Water poured over the lower deck and into the fire box, so that when we finally arrived at the foot of the rapids into good water, the ship had no power. Luck was with us however, and just as the anchor was thrown overboard, we landed bow first on a sandbar.

"The fireman and engineer soon got a fire started again under the boiler and in less than two hours we were back at the foot of the rapids, ready for another try, the captain as unperturbed as though the whole matter had been routine. The next try we fastened to a larger tree and had no further difficulty."

phew—phew—phew.

"On the whole a sternwheeler was a pretty noisy contraption. In addition to the steam screeching from the stack, there was a continuous slap-slap-slap as each bucket on the paddlewheel hit the water. The vessels had a deep-toned, baying type of whistle which frequently added to the uproar. Then if everything wasn't going right the mate or captain would contribute a lively selection of comments, thus adding a personal touch to the din.

"To me, a sternwheeler slapping her way through whitewater rapids, spray cascading from bow and paddlewheel, steam and smoke belching skyward in great swirls of black and white was a picture that once seen was never forgotten."

Since sternwheelers brought to isolated communities mail and supplies, new faces and a link with the outside, their arrival was looked forward to and frequently the cause of excitement. In May 1911, the B.X. produced more of a flurry at Quesnel than usual. Her whistle blast caused a dray team owned by George Johnson to bolt, with George "pluckily

holding onto the lines, and riding out the storm." Then a stagehorse coming down the gangplank fell into the river. Embarrassed by this sudden dunking it galloped off and was two miles down the Cariboo Road when captured. Then a cow "created no end of antics before it was finally forced to a corner of a corral fence near the landing." Some Indian girls on horseback had been watching the white man's show in silent but obvious amusement, then the whistle shrilled again. One horse bucked and "rider, saddle and blankets went about six feet into the air, and landed a few paces away." Afterwards the vessel churned away and calm returned.

In addition to providing a reliable link to the outside world

At left the Revelstoke on the Columbia River, while below the Inlander leaves a white wake on salt water near Prince Rupert. At bottom left sternwheelers fight ice in Lower Arrow Lake in 1890 and the B.C. Express challenges the Grand Canyon of the Upper Fraser not far from Mt. Robson.

for those settling the frontier, sternwheelers had another valuable trait—they were adaptable. When their usefulness ended in one region, they were often taken to another. At times this transfer was not without problems. In East Kootenay the *Gwendoline* fell off a railway flatcar into a canyon and was wrecked. The *Moyie* and the *Minto* were shipped from Toronto to the Kootenays, each in 1,000 pieces, while in 1863 boilers and other ironware for the *Enterprise* on Upper Fraser were packed by mules some 300 miles from Port Douglas. This journey was a tribute to pioneer ingenuity, but then so was the method used to transport boilers for the *Lady of the Lake* on Anderson Lake, and the *Champion* on Seton Lake. They arrived at Port Douglas in five sections and were rolled over 68 miles of rough trail.

Since pioneer sternwheelers were built of lumber, basic material was no problem. If there was no sawmill around, lumber was cut by hand, but boiler and engines weren't so available. For this reason some vessels had rather unorthodox means of propulsion.

The *Kamloops* on the Thompson-Shuswap waterway had a power plant originally used in 1867 in a flour mill at Soda Creek in Cariboo. The contraption, though noisy, was serviceable. In fact, from the *Kamloops* it was later transferred to a new vessel, the *Spallumcheen*. The *Clive* on Columbia River got her boiler from a steam plough once used in Manitoba, while the *Nowitka* on the same river had an engine from a Montreal ferry. The *Henrietta* even got along without an engine. Since her hull was completed before her engines, her owner, Captain William Moore, had her towed up the Fraser River to Harrison Lake and operated her under sail until the power plant was ready.

Usual fuel for sternwheelers was wood, but coal, oil, or anything else combustible could be substituted, including bacon which an exasperated Lower Fraser River skipper used in a vain attempt to outsteam a rival. Fuel consumption varied, but a hard-working vessel could use a pile eight feet high by eight feet long by four wide in half an hour. The Hudson's Bay Company's *Beaver*, first paddlewheeler on the Pacific Coast, carried six woodcutters. Even at that her progress was in spurts since she burned in one day what her fuel suppliers cut in two.

The *Beaver* was launched on the Thames River near London on May 2, 1835. She wasn't large, just over 100 feet long by 20 wide, 109 tons burden with two, 35 horse-power engines and a 6½-foot-wide paddlewheel on each side just forward of amidships. She was, however, pound for pound probably the strongest vessel afloat.

Her keel was elm, her ribs English oak, her planking oak and African teak, fastened to the frames with copper bolts. Internally she was just as sturdy, with oak and teak lining, reinforced with heavy iron straps that were also fastened to the frame with copper bolts. She was, in the words of the

surveyor who examined her for her Certificate of Registry, issued May 6, 1835, "Well constructed and workmanship generally of the highest quality."

She arrived at the Columbia River on a spring morning in March 1836, having made the passage from England around Cape Horn under sail. She sailed up the Columbia to Fort Vancouver, arriving April 10, 225 days after leaving England. At the Fort her paddlewheels were installed and she started a career that lasted over 50 years. She became familiar with the waters of the entire Pacific Northwest, carrying supplies to isolated forts and trading posts and exploring scores of bays and inlets from Puget Sound to Alaska. She brought horses, wild Spanish cattle and supplies to the southern tip of Vancouver Island in 1843 when Fort Victoria was established, and on a wet November 19, 1858, she carried Governor Douglas, Judge Matthew Baillie Begbie and other dignitaries to Fort Langley to officiate at the birth of the Crown Colony of British Columbia.

But by an oddity of history, while she pioneered steam

The Okanagan on Okanagan Lake about 1908. A sternwheeler excursion on lake or river was a popular event during pioneer days. A typical outing was described in the Fort George Herald on September 11, 1911: "The British Columbia Express Company's big steamboat B.X. left here this morning with the South Fort George baseball team on board, and a party of excursionists from this place to witness the ball game to be played at Quesnel. . . ."

navigation on 110 miles of the Columbia, an American river, it was American paddlewheelers which first ventured up a similar distance of the Fraser, a British river. For this reason British Columbia's sternwheel heritage was patterned not on British conservatism but on a wild west legacy from Oregon and California.

Steamboating in California has been described as colorful, a true though modest statement. For instance, during the 1850's in the Sacramento-San Francisco Bay areas alone over 200 people died on paddlewheelers, the disasters frequently caused by boilers blowing up while vessels were racing. In B.C. these explosions were duplicated, but more modestly, and only a few dozen passengers and crew died in the wrecks.

During California steamboat races some passengers became so spirited they took pot shots at rival vessels. In B.C. passengers were less excitable, although in 1882 when *Gertrude* and *William Irving* were rivals on the Lower Fraser River, someone heaved an egg at the latter's skipper. The

Victoria Colonist commented: "The rivalry on the river is becoming fast and furious, and we would advise caution on all sides, for should a disaster occur, a terrible responsibility will attach somewhere." Later, on the Skeena River, a race almost led to the terrible responsibility mentioned by the paper when the master of *Mount Royal* left his helm while in a rapids to get a rifle to shoot his rival. Then on the Upper Fraser River there was almost a disaster when the captain of *Conveyor* deliberately rammed the B.X. while the vessels were racing.

In California during a race, engineers jammed the safety valve with an anvil or anything heavy. In B.C. the technique was a little more refined. In 1881 on the Lower Fraser River the captain of the *Western Slope*, William Moore, and his chief engineer were each fined $200 for jamming the safety valve with a wedge. The method, however, tended to vary with the skipper.

On Stikine River in 1898 author Guy Lawrence was a passenger on the sternwheeler *Skagit Chief*. Of the voyage, Mr. Lawrence wrote: "After two unsuccessful tries to beat up a rapid, the captain was in a state of frenzy. We heard him shouting down to the engine room for more steam. Finally, when he had tried vainly to pass the rock a third time he left the wheelhouse to the pilot and rushed down to the engine room. Seizing a large spanner, he screwed the safety valve of the boiler down and stood over the two firemen, urging them to keep piling on more fuel. Then he rushed back to the wheelhouse."

With the safety valve screwed tight the vessel again headed upstream, but then someone shouted "man overboard." It was the chief engineer. He had jumped into the river rather than stay on a vessel he felt was about to explode. He was rescued but the *Skagit Chief* never did make the rapid.

Another trait B.C. steamboatmen inherited from San Francisco was desire for a monopoly to ensure high freight rates. Even the lofty H.B.C. accepted $1,000 a month to keep the *Beaver* off the Fraser, but then on Skeena River paid a rival $2,500 to keep his vessel on the ways. As early as 1859 owners of the sternwheelers *Governor Douglas* and *Colonel Moody* petitioned Governor Douglas "to grant to us the exclusive right to navigate with Steam Boats the Fraser and Harrison Rivers from New Westminster to Port Douglas and to Fort Hope for one year." They suggested what they felt was "a fair compensation for the steamers" but Douglas disallowed the petition because desired "fair compensation" was far too high.

Another method by which owners attempted to ensure a monopoly is revealed by the experience of the *Umatilla*, pioneer sternwheeler on the Lower Fraser River. She was an American vessel that arrived in 1858 but remained only two

---

Sternwheelers always responded to a white flag, as at upper left, pulling ashore for a full cargo or a prospector bent on a spree. They also raced at the slightest challenge. The International and the Moyie, at left, churn the West Arm of Kootenay Lake in 1899.

One old-timer thought a sternwheeler's whistle, opposite, was "between the growl of a bear and the hoot of a great horned owl...." A contrasting opinion was that it was like a bagpipe, best heard from a distance.

months, being replaced by the *Maria*. The switch, as one writer phrased it, "revealed the cuteness of the Americans." The *Maria* had originally been bought from the California Steam Navigation Company which had a monopoly on the Sacramento River. Terms of the sale stipulated that she be kept off the Sacramento, but nothing mentioned the *Umatilla*. Consequently, the owners simply traded vessels, taking the *Umatilla* from the Fraser to San Francisco and forcing the California Steam Navigation Company to buy her to maintain their monopoly. This practice was later followed whenever possible by B.C. sternwheel owners.

While monopolies and races were a colorful, if hazardous, phase of sternwheel days, they weren't the only newsworthy aspect. Vessels themselves were at times unpredictable, beginning with the *Governor Douglas*, first sternwheeler built on Vancouver Island.

She was scheduled for launching at Fort Victoria on October 30, 1858. Among those present were Governor Douglas, Admiral Baynes, and assorted other notables. At 2 o'clock all was ready: blocks knocked free, crowd ready to cheer, cannon primed to fire a salute, the Governor's young daughter, Agnes, nervously waiting to perform the christening. The *Governor Douglas*, unfortunately, wasn't impressed by the fuss. She sat on the ways, as still as a broody hen.

While dignitaries stared silently at the motionless vessel, workmen hastily attached ropes and tugged. She didn't budge. Then anchors were taken into the bay and the vessel pulled towards them. She trembled then began to move. Champagne splattered, people cheered, cannon boomed, the vessel slid slowly forward. Her bow hit the water and the crowd took a breath to cheer anew, but the bashful *Governor Douglas* refused to dip her stern into the water.

This time the crowd joined the workmen in the tugging, but she refused to budge. Finally the attempt was abandoned and spectators turned to the champagne and other refreshments. But, commented one newspaper, ". . . everything passed off with diminished spirits in consequence of

The Hazelton in shallow water on the Skeena River in 1910. Secret of a sternwheeler's remarkable success was the fact that the bow could be ashore while the paddlewheel remained in water deep enough to provide power—even though the "deep" water was at times remarkably shallow. The paddlewheel was usually 16 to 24 feet in diameter with paddles immersed six to eighteen inches, depending on the vessel. Besides providing propulsion, the paddlewheel had

other uses. For instance in 1862 the Fraser River froze from Lulu Island to Hope, with ice in places two feet thick. New Westminster was isolated from December to March 12 when Captain Moore smashed a passage with his Flying Dutchman. He attacked the ice paddlewheel first, and was three days breaking the blockade. To show their appreciation, New Westminster residents subscribed some $400 to repair the Dutchman's badly damaged paddlewheel.

the unexpected failure of the launch." Not until eleven that night, coaxed by a schooner pulling her, did the *Governor Douglas* reluctantly become water-borne.

But the unusual wasn't present only at launchings. Passage on a sternwheeler frequently meant more than simply travelling between ports of departure and destination. Among other things, the vessels caught fire, blew up, impaled themselves on snags, tore open their hulls on rocks, and bashed into each other. The latter fate ended the career of the sidewheeler *Enterprise*. Just off Victoria on July 28, 1885 she collided with the sternwheeler *R. P. Rithet*—in open water on a smooth sea in broad daylight and clear weather.

After the collision the *Victoria Colonist* reported that: "Terrible confusion and a perfect babble ensued. The Chinese and Indians on both steamers sent forth unearthly yells . . . ladies went into hysterics . . . many men jumped clear of the *Enterprise* and swam to the *Rithet*, several who could not swim or were afraid to try it jumped in and seized floating bales of hay. To add to the confusion several cattle

were observed swimming around, one of whom jumped into the ladies' cabin of the *Enterprise*."

Despite the fact that men, women and children were knocked or jumped into the cold water, only two drowned. The cattle weren't so fortunate, with 24 of 27 head perishing. Captain Insley of the *R. P. Rithet* was held responsible since he left a green hand in the wheelhouse while he went

---

Each waterway presented its own problems. At lower left is the Enterprise *after her collision, while below the* Operator *after being hit by a falling tree on the Skeena River. At bottom left the* Spokane *burns in Kaslo Bay in 1895 and on the right the wrecked* Kaslo *near Ainsworth. On May 27, 1910 as she was docking a wave threw her stern on a submerged pile. She was holed, then beached to prevent a boiler explosion. Snags, or dead trees, were a problem on rivers. They lodged on bars and the tips, honed by silty water, became spear points. In early days they even got names, often that of the vessel which rammed them.*

below for lunch. He had his license suspended.

On the Lower Fraser River in 1858 weather was unusually frigid and on December 9 the *Enterprise* was frozen in between Fort Hope and Fort Langley. Since she had neither provisions nor accommodation, many passengers decided to walk overland to Fort Langley, even though most had no food, blankets, nor proper clothing. Three days later the weather moderated and the *Enterprise* was chopped free. Captain Wright steamed up and down the river shore, blowing his whistle and eventually rescuing all passengers. The *Victoria Gazette* later reported: "Many . . . had some of their limbs frozen—others have their feet and hands frost-bitten, and all agree in saying that they experienced the most intense and horrible suffering it is possible to conceive."

In the same paper was a card of thanks from the passengers to Captain Wright: "We . . . beg to tender to Capt. Thomas Wright, of the steamer *Enterprise*, plying on Fraser River, our deep heartfelt acknowledgements for his humanity and Christian benevolence, in rescuing from destruction 110 men, 1 woman and 3 children lost in the snow on the intricate route and almost impassable woods of Fraser River. . . . We feel that, but for our unexpected deliverance, the pall of death must have been stretched over us all. . . ."

Emphasizing the truth of the last statement was the fact that in the Valley during the cold spell four men and a woman did freeze to death.

Not all diversions, fortunately, were potentially tragic. In 1887 two Englishmen, J. Lees and W. Clutterbuck, were aboard the *Duchess* on Upper Columbia River when a mink swam by. In their book *A Ramble in British Columbia* they noted that the captain "with sportsmanlike spirit beyond all praise, undertook to run it down with the swift and elegant *Duchess*, a proceeding somewhat akin to setting an elephant to catch black beetles in a black kitchen." Passengers and crew nevertheless hurried to the bow, one optimist clutching a landing net. The mink escaped unharmed, but not some of the onlookers who were knocked flat by the stout limb of a low-hanging fir.

The Charlotte sliding sideways through Cottonwood Canyon on the Fraser River 18 miles north of Quesnel. On underpowered vessels, passengers walked around the more dangerous canyons of the Fraser and Skeena. Traces of the footpaths are still evident, overgrown with grass and moss, littered with deadfalls, but once important links in B.C.'s development. At upper right an unknown sternwheeler at an unknown landing, although the latter could be on the Fraser near Yale in the late 1860's.

The B.C. Express "wooding up." Since sternwheelers gobbled up to five cords an hour, wooding stops were frequent, with about four cords at a time piled on the foredeck. The wood, cut in winter by contract, was a valuable income for pioneer farmers and ranchers. Some piles were immense, one left on the Skeena when steamboating ended contained 1,000 cords—a pile 4 feet high by 4 feet wide by almost 1½ miles long.

Of the vessel, they noted that she presented a somewhat decrepit appearance, as "about a fortnight before our arrival she had been wrecked in the Columbia with a full cargo and some passengers. They had managed to fish her up again out of about fourteen feet of water, and she was now in steaming order, but her fittings and former smartness were gone."

For sternwheelers, however, sinking was an occupational hazard that was usually only a temporary inconvenience. But considering obstacles that the vessels faced, the wonder isn't that they sank, but that they appeared at all.

British Columbia's rivers are generally wild and unfriendly, whelped by mountains among the world's most rugged: Rocky, Babine, Monashee, Coast, Selkirk, Purcell, Stikine, Cariboo, and other slab-sided ramparts where winter snowfall can exceed 50 feet and Pacific storms dump rain by millions of tons. They are broken by whirlpool-filled canyons and rock-toothed rapids, in spring adrift with debris, in autumn laced with bars and shallows, in winter running ice floes which overnight can freeze from bank to bank, or rasp jagged holes in a sternwheeler's hull.

Many lakes the vessels plied are inland seas, mountain-ringed troughs where storms arise with the suddenness of an opening door and spume from waves curled high over a sternwheeler's pilothouse. Then there was B.C.'s reef-broken, deeply incised coast, its deadly nature emphasized by the hundreds of people who have its fog-shrouded waters as a grave.

But it wasn't the hazards of river and lake and ocean that defeated the sternwheelers; it was the roads and railroads that they in many cases made possible. Vessels and their crews bowed not to counteracting forces but to progress. They can have no finer memorial.

High on a nearly completed pier of the Grand Trunk Pacific railway bridge over the Skeena River in 1911, workmen pause to watch a sternwheeler sail slowly by. Her job completed, she drops downstream to oblivion.

CHAPTER TWO

Lower Fraser River
PART ONE

British Columbia sternwheel days dawned on the Fraser River during the rousing days of the 1858 gold rush. It was a spectacular period of spirits by the barrel and nuggets by the ton, of wedged safety valves and searing boiler explosions, of captains rich one week, bankrupt the next, and of vessels summarized by a skipper who stated that one sternwheeler "may do well for passengers, but I wouldn't trust treasure in her."

On August 3, 1861, an editorial in the *Victoria Colonist* noted: "Within the last 18 months, we have had three of our steamboats blown up. Two became total wrecks; one the hull was saved. The loss of life through these explosions has been from 20 to 25 persons, and nearly or quite as many have been seriously wounded. A loss of property cannot be less than from $70,000 to $80,000. Such a fearful loss of life and property, besides personal injuries, ought to direct public attention to a careful consideration of the causes that lead to such catastrophes. . . ."

Causes of the catastrophes included incompetent crews, absence of safety regulations, and unseaworthy vessels. Inferior metal in the boiler was frequently blamed, although boilers were not always at fault. Since the fastest vessel was the most popular—and profitable—steam pressure was kept high. "We raced another steamer all the way down . . ." noted a miner named C. F. Morrison while travelling from Yale to New Westminster during the gold rush. "The Captain came down from the pilothouse every now and then to look at the steam, saying 'Don't carry too much steam, Chris, but beat that boat!' which Chris did, carrying, I believe, a little too much steam when the captain was out of sight."

In the early 1860's English author R. Byron Johnson travelled on a sternwheeler bound to Hope. A rival vessel overtook them and the captain ordered more steam. Still the rival gained, and, noted the author, "Several sacks of bacon were thrown into the flames, making them roar like a strong

The Onward, *photographed between 1867-69. Light, she sailed in 13 inches of water, with another inch for each ton of freight. She arrived at New Westminster on her maiden voyage August 1865, the "big gun on Pioneer Wharf being fired in honour . . . ."*

east wind. Up went the steam gauge till it showed 160 lbs. to the square inch, just 40 more than was allowed by the government certificate, framed and glazed in the cabin."

When the engineer pointed to the steam gauge, the Captain replied, ". . . the old boat's never bin whipped yet, and ain't going to be til she busts!"

Shortly afterwards she shuddered to a stop, impaled on a snag which speared through hull, ten feet of cargo, and an unfortunate horse. The rival churned by, passengers cheering and "without stopping to see if we were sinking or not." The hole was plugged with blankets commandeered from passengers and the vessel ran ashore. Here passengers had to wait for two days for rescue since no rival vessel would stop.

This intense rivalry, moreover, wasn't restricted to stern-wheelers. Victoria and New Westminster, capitals of the Crown Colonies of Vancouver Island and of British Columbia, fought bitterly. "A pimple on the face of creation," Victoria once summed up New Westminster. "Built on a frog-pond," was New Westminster's opinion of Victoria. Yale, on the Fraser River, and Port Douglas, on Harrison Lake, competed for supremacy as supply point to Cariboo. Finally, sternwheel owners and merchants warred over shipping costs, with exasperated businessmen at times building their own vessels in defence against monopolistic freight rates.

Main setting for this saga was the last 110 miles of the Fraser River from Yale, then some 75 miles of salt water to Victoria. From Yale by 1865 a 12-foot-wide wagon road wandered some 400 miles northward through rock, fir, and mountain wilderness to Cariboo gold fields. Trails from this lonely swath fingered northward to Omineca, westward to Chilcotin, eastward to Kamloops Lake and Columbia River. Then to the south the Dewdney Trail roller-coastered 360 miles from Hope east to the Kootenays. But as the out-thrust twig is connected to the tree trunk, so were roads and trails connected with the river. Southern terminus was Victoria, half-way was New Westminster; at its head were Port Douglas and Yale.

First of the gold rush flotilla was the sidewheeler *Surprise*, owned by the California Steam Navigation Company. She nosed into the Fraser River at 1:30 p.m. on June 5, 1858. That night she anchored some 16 miles above Fort Langley, and reached Fort Hope at 2 p.m. next day. The miners celebrated her arrival in a manner that became traditional—setting off gunpowder for firecrackers and happily swigging toasts, "on the strength of which most of them got drunk."

On June 8 another American sidewheeler, the *Sea Bird*, started upstream. She was underpowered and after struggling two days finally landed her impatient passengers a mile below Fort Hope. Next trip she reached Hope, although the *Victoria Gazette* noted: "Her progress up is reported to have been of the most curious character, sometimes the current would get the better of the battle and the steamer would

drift astern despite herself." On her return she rammed an island. For over two months Captain John T. Wright struggled to refloat her, while the *Surprise* passed back and forth, earning something like $250,000. Captain Wright's only consolation was that the island was named after his vessel.

The *Sea Bird*, however, wasn't finished with misfortune. On September 7 she burned up with the loss of two lives—first paddlewheel victims in a region eventually called British Columbia. In forthcoming years they would be joined by many other passengers and vessels.

The *Sea Bird's* survivors were rescued by the *Wilson G. Hunt* and taken to Fort Langley. Among them was an Austrian professor, Dr. Carl Friesach, who continued his trip on the sternwheeler *Umatilla*. Of his upstream voyage, Dr. Friesach wrote: ". . . the boat . . . did not contain any cabins and even mattresses and blankets were lacking; the floor of the saloon was so covered with coal dust that it was impossible to lie down without getting very dirty. Moreover the passengers, who were mostly miners, were so numerous that it was difficult to find sleeping room. Finally two of us lay down on the dining table, another under it. . . ."

When they passed the mountains near present day Chilliwack they ". . . were prevented from enjoying the beautiful landscape by a strong wind, which, blowing in the direction of our course, caused the sparks from the smokestack to fall all about us, burning holes in our hats and clothes."

The *Umatilla* was the pioneer sternwheeler on the Fraser, arriving at Victoria from Columbia River July 13, 1858. On the Columbia she had the misfortune to plummet over a rapids on her maiden voyage, killing a passenger. On the Fraser, however, she was more fortunate. Besides being the first sternwheeler on the river, she was first to explore Harrison River and Lake and first to reach Yale. When she arrived at the upriver community on July 21 an eyewitness wrote: "The town was thrown into a high state of excitement, upon hearing the screeching of a steam-whistle, and a rumor gaining circulation that a little sternwheeler was on her way up the river. Everybody was soon on the lookout . . . and canoes were sent beyond the bend of the river . . . to ascertain the truth of the report. Soon we learned by the shoutings along the banks of the river and the continuous discharge of guns and pistols, that the report was true; whereupon, there was the greatest rejoicing and pleasure manifested by everyone, and powder was burnt amidst the wildest excitement. . . ."

The second sternwheeler to arrive on Fraser River was the *Enterprise*. Originally built for service on the Willamette River in Oregon, she was bought by Captain Wright and sent north. Crossing the treacherous bar at the mouth of Columbia River she was badly battered and sank. She was refloated and eventually reached the Fraser, where she was very successful, earning $25,000 for one trip between Victoria and Murderer's Bar near Hope.

In fact with the exception of the unfortunate *Sea Bird*, the summer of 1858 was profitable for both sidewheelers and sternwheelers. They carried thousands of miners up the Fraser, then promptly brought them back again. Most of the miners arrived when the river was in flood, bars awash not in nuggets but glacial water. With a cry of "Fraser River, Humbug" the majority returned to Victoria and the United States.

By late autumn only two vessels remained on the Fraser. They were the *Enterprise* and the *Maria*, the latter having replaced the pioneer *Umatilla*. Their owners then taught customers the fundamentals of profitable steamboat operation. Freight rates that in June were $4 to $7 a ton from

New Westminster between 1865-70 and the Wilson G. Hunt. This sidewheeler, built in 1849 for the Coney Island excursion trade, came to California around Cape Horn during the gold rush. She took 322 days, nearly foundering on the way, but making amends by netting over $1 million in a season. Capable of carrying 300 passengers, she arrived on the Fraser River in 1858 but soon returned to San Francisco, then came back next year. Afterwards she returned to the U.S. again but in 1877 was purchased by Captain Irving and plied the Victoria-New Westminster route. When she arrived the local paper noted: "The appearance of the vessel is . . . most imposing . . . the new paint and gilding make her look as trim as if she had been just turned out of a mold . . . ."

Victoria to Hope became $60. Coffee, butter, and bacon at Yale cost $1 a pound; beans that were three cents a pound in Victoria were .75 cents at Lytton; mailing a letter from Yale to Victoria was $1.

There were rumours that Governor Douglas planned to force a rate reduction but nothing happened. The *Victoria Gazette* did comment: ". . . though opposed in general to arbitrary action on the part of officials, there appears to be no other means of bringing rapacious steamboat owners to reason."

As people would learn, only one factor lowered fares— competition. On September 8, 1858 promise of competition appeared with launching of the sidewheeler *Caledonia* at Victoria, first steam vessel built north of the U.S. Pacific Coast. "She slid off the ways into the water quite easily," noted the *Victoria Gazette* proudly, "and took to the waters as naturally as a duck. . . ." Unfortunately, she had a trait not found in a duck, and it was later to sadden all Victoria.

Another new vessel launched at Victoria was *Governor Douglas*, the sternwheeler which caused so much embarrassment when she refused to leave the ways. The two craft reflected the profound changes that had occurred on Vancouver Island and the Mainland in five months. In an area where wages were $80 a year, suddenly over $2,000,000 had poured in. From a lonely fur trading post Victoria became a pulsing community of several thousand people with businesses that included saloons, hotels, shipyards, and many others.

On the Mainland, changes were even more dramatic. Into an area unknown except to a few H.B.C. employees poured thousands of gold seekers. They surged up the Fraser, battled through her canyons, then disappeared into the silence of her hosts of tributary waterways. Because of the influx, on November 19, 1858, the area officially became the Crown Colony of British Columbia. Its capital was Derby, later replaced by a community called first Queensborough, then New Westminster.

During 1858 the Fraser yielded some $2,000,000 in treasure, although of 25,000 miners who surged north, only 3,000 remained by winter. But spring of 1859 brought thousands back, in addition to two new sternwheelers—*Henrietta*, and *Colonel Moody*, sister to the *Governor Douglas*. The latter two vessels were owned by the Victoria Steam Navigation Company, a firm which included Captain William Irving, pioneer steamboatman from Columbia River. He was to become the most famous of all gold rush skippers.

The *Henrietta* was built for Captain William Moore, a pioneer as optimistic as daybreak. He bobbed through five decades of B.C.'s history like a log in a rapid—now submerged, now riding the crest in triumph. He explored the province, built packtrails and pioneered rivers, won and lost several fortunes, and battled Irving and later Irving's son in the rate wars which flared as shipping companies fought for supremacy.

First of these wars erupted during the 1859 season. By September, freight between New Westminster and Victoria had dropped from $12 a ton to .50 cents; fare from $10 to .50 cents. On September 22 the *Victoria Gazette* suggested tersely: "Now is the time to forward supplies to the mining regions for the coming winter."

The mining regions referred to had extended during the summer over 500 miles northward. The Fraser Canyon, described as "utterly impassable for any animal but a man, a goat, or a dog" had been by-passed by a route from Harrison River through a series of lakes and rivers to Lillooet. But the route wasn't popular since freight and passengers had to transfer from boat to wagon and wagon to boat seven times in 116 miles. For this reason miners celebrated when a sternwheeler fought a few miles further up the Fraser.

On February 19, 1860, there was a grand celebration in Yale when Captain Moore arrived in the *Henrietta*, first sternwheeler to venture to the community since the *Umatilla* 19 months before. "All was excitement which I have never witnessed in Yale," wrote a correspondent. ". . . anvils were made to answer the purpose of cannon and quite a brisk firing was kept up all afternoon. A large banner was displayed on the river front upon which the words 'Welcome Henrietta' but echoed the heartfelt sentiment of the entire community. Captain Moore deserves much credit for his untiring energy and perseverance."

A few days after *Henrietta* arrived at Yale, the *Victoria Colonist* reported with dismay that during the winter the British Columbia Steam Navigation Company had also been persevering—but for a different reason. They had arranged that only British-made vessels could trade on Harrison River, main portal to upriver diggings. By a coincidence their vessels were the only ones which met the new regulations. "Excellent scheme," noted the paper sarcastically. "Free trade exploded—monopoly the real thing after all. It avoids competition. We congratulate the B.C.S.N. Co. on their success."

Three sternwheelers which appeared in 1860 were the *Marzelle* for Lillooet Lake, *Lady of the Lake* for Anderson Lake, and *Champion* for Seton Lake, the three major waterways forming part of the route which bypassed the Fraser Canyon. The trio were small and underpowered, although at least one of them made up in freight rates what she lacked in size. "The beautiful little steamer called the *Marzelle* is now running regularly on Lillooet Lake," wrote a *Victoria Colonist* correspondent on July 18, 1860. "She is owned by parties, who but for their cupidity, would certainly deserve credit for their enterprise. They think they have the monopoly of the Lake, and demand higher prices for freight than has hitherto been charged by small boats. In fact, their demands are so exorbitant, that parties have again put on small boats; so that under present circumstances the steamer is rather an injury than a benefit to the route."

Later in the season the *Victoria Colonist* was more cheerful, noting with satisfaction: "We have already built and navigating the Fraser between New Westminster and Fort Hope and Port Douglas, the steamboats *Governor Douglas*, *Colonel Moody*, and *Maria*. . . . Then we have the steamers, *Otter*, *Wilson G. Hunt*, and *Caledonia* running from Victoria to the river. . . . Then there is the *Henrietta* who will resume her trips on the first. . . . Add to these the boats now building, the *Hope*, the *Flying Dutchman*, the *Fort Yale*, and the sidewheel constructing for Captain Jamieson; and the *Beaver* . . . and we shall have a perfect fleet of steamboats ready for service by the 1st of November. Twelve steamboats in the hands of eight distinct companies, and all in good order, is no mean force. . . . All this competition we feel assured, will assist materially in populating our sister colony, and in benefitting Victoria."

Two vessels under construction were the result of an attempt by the British Columbia Steam Navigation Company to reduce opposition. In a move typical of the period, they paid Captain Moore to withdraw his *Henrietta* from the river. There was, however, nothing in the agreement preventing Captain Moore from selling her, which he did. Since the new owners had no contract with Irving, they promptly put *Henrietta* back in service. Moore, meanwhile, started building a new vessel, the *Flying Dutchman*.

Then a group of Yale businessmen decided to do something about the high freight rates. They formed the Yale Steam Navigation Company and ordered a sternwheeler built at Victoria. The $31,000 vessel, the *Fort Yale,* arrived at Yale on her maiden voyage on November 26, 1860. She was received ". . . with every manifestation of rejoicing. . . . Cannons and anvils were fired, and British and American flags hoisted . . . a dinner was held, and the dancing continued till an early hour in the morning."

She made the return trip to New Westminster in 7½ hours, a new record. On December 26 she set another record, one most welcome to lonely bachelors. Among her passengers was the first single white woman to arrive at Yale. A few months later, the *Fort Yale* was again in the news, although for a more tragic reason.

On April 14, at Union Bar some two miles above Hope, she blew up. So great was the blast that a 90-pound chunk of boiler was blown a quarter mile inland. "TERRIBLE CATASTROPHE" said a headline in the *Victoria Colonist* at Victoria, where flags were lowered to half mast.

An eye-witness account was given by a passenger, H. Lee Alley: "The noise resembled, together with the crash, a heavy blow upon a sharp-sounding Chinese gong. The cabin floor raised and then fell in; at the same time the hurricane roof fell upon us, cutting our heads more or less, and blocking up all means of escape forward of the dinner table. We quickly made for the windows and doors in the after-part of the cabin, and got on the roof of the hurricane house, and there beheld a scene that baffles all description, and such as I trust I may never witness again. The boat, but a few seconds before nobly bucking against the swift current, was now a sinking mass of ruins from stem to stern—scarcely anything remained in sight above water, but a small portion of her bow and the after part of her saloon, and those gradually disappearing below water. Five or six human beings, their faces streaming with blood, and presenting an awful appearance, were struggling for life."

The shattered vessel was swept below Hope where survivors were rescued. Five white men, including her captain, Smith Jamieson, and an unknown number of Indians and Chinese died in the wreck. Among survivors was James Ellison. He had been in the pilothouse with Captain Jamieson, and since the pilothouse was almost directly over the boiler, it received the full force of the blast. Ellison was blown high in the air but landed in the water with only bruises. Another passenger, Samuel Powers, wasn't so fortunate. He was also blown high in the air, but landed on shore and was killed. No trace was ever found of 26-year-old Captain Jamieson.

Other survivors included purser F. J. Barnard and Captain William Irving, who was a passenger. Shortly before the explosion, he was in the pilothouse with Captain Jamieson and offered to steer while Jamieson ate. Jamieson laughingly remarked that he would not trust his boat to an opposition pilot. Irving went below and just sat down to dinner when the vessel was demolished.

Captain Smith Jamieson was a Scot, one of six brothers, five of whom came to the Pacific Northwest. All became steamboatmen, with tragic results. Smith was the third to die in steamboat mishaps on Columbia and Fraser Rivers. The other two brothers were also to die in a paddlewheel explosion.

Loss of the *Fort Yale* left six sternwheelers: *Governor Douglas, Colonel Moody,* and *Maria* operated by Captain Irving's company; *Flying Dutchman* and *Hope* by Captain W. Moore; and *Henrietta* by Captain Millard. All were engaged in brutal competition. Freight from New Westminster to Douglas was $1 a ton, passage free. "The cheaper the freights and the rates of passage, the better for both colonies," said the *Victoria Colonist* on May 21, 1861, in almost a gleeful tone.

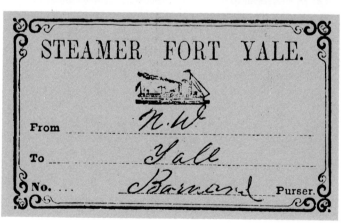

STEAMER FORT YALE.

From ... *N.W*

To ... *Yale*

No. ... *Barnard* Purser.

Recovered from the wreck of the Fort Yale, this ticket is signed by purser F. J. Barnard, at top. He survived the explosion then founded the famous B.C. Express Company which in 1865 alone hauled $4.5 million in gold from Cariboo mines to Yale. Barnard later became a Federal member of parliament and a prominent B.C. citizen.

The owners didn't agree with this theory. They "held a meeting" and on June 12 the paper announced: "The various steamboat lines on Fraser River formed a combination, and freight will be taken to Douglas henceforth at $15 a ton; to Yale, $25 a ton." Shortly afterward, freight to Douglas increased another $10 a ton, a lesson in addition dismaying to businessmen at Douglas and Lillooet, among them Gustavus Blin Wright who was soon to build most of the famous Cariboo Wagon Road.

At a Victoria shipyard lay a vessel intended to be a sister to *Fort Yale* but never completed. Douglas-Lillooet businessmen formed a company and purchased the hull. By August she was ready. Freight rates dropped from $25 to $5 a ton to Douglas, from $25 to $10 to Yale.

Meanwhile, in lonely wilderness to the north, miners explored the Fraser and her tributaries. They poled crude rafts up side streams and lakes, tested gravel on creeks and valleys inumerable, fought their way to the roof of the land. In a country that became known as Cariboo, they found the rainbow's pot of gold. An editorial in the June 12, 1861 *Victoria Colonist* noted: "Men don't like to state how rich they are, from a fear of being guilty of telling incredible stories. Neither do we wish to overdraw the picture. . . . Yet facts are stubborn things, and there is no denying that the Antler Creek, Snowshoe, Cunninghams Creek, Keithley's, Quesnelle

Yale, believed taken in the late 1860's. From here freight to Cariboo and other points was packed by mules or loaded into freight wagons. Oxen were commonly used for pulling, with a return trip to Barkerville taking up to three months.

Liquor was a major item of freight, with the May 7, 1862 Victoria Colonist noting: "Great complaint is made against the merchants on both routes (Douglas and Yale) because of their action in sending forward . . . liquor at a time when the necessaries of life are so scarce, and threats to stave kegs containing spirits are not infrequently heard from half-starved miners who anxiously await the arrival of provisions to enable them to prosecute their journey to the mines."

River diggings, are unsurpassed as gold districts."

Shortly afterward, the same paper headlined another steamboat disaster. On August 3 the sidewheeler *Cariboo* exploded in Victoria harbor, killing six people and seven horses. The vessel, intended to replace the *Fort Yale,* had just completed her maiden voyage. "The beautiful steamer," reported the *Victoria Colonist,* "was found nothing but a floating hulk, ripped and tore from stern to stern, and floating outward with the receding tide."

Flags in Victoria were lowered to half mast and business houses closed. One passenger killed was Paul De Garro. In 1858 on a small hand press he had printed *The Fraser Mines Vindicated,* first book published in the Colony. Among others killed were assistant engineer James Jamieson and Captain Archibald Jamieson—four and fifth Jamieson brothers to die in steamboat mishaps.

Not long after the *Cariboo* explosion, paddlewheelers again made headlines, although for a less tragic reason. Gold was flowing from Cariboo, with over $200,000 brought to Victoria on a single vessel. News of these riches spread around the world, and in spring 1862, over 4,000 men surged up the Fraser, while hundreds more trekked overland through Okanagan. Optimistic reports of additional strikes in Okanagan and Shuswap, Peace River and Stikine spurred them forward. Supplies and men poured into Douglas and Yale, there to begin a 400-mile journey to the Cariboo creeks. To provide easier access, work started on a wagon road through the Fraser Canyon, while to the north G. B. Wright hewed a 140-mile section from Clinton to Soda Creek.

Despite the surge of business, a rate war erupted. The *Flying Dutchman* and the *Union* offered passage from New Westminster to Douglas for $1; *Hope* and *Henrietta* countered with 50 cents, horses and mules free; while *Colonel Moody* carried passengers free and included meals. The ruinous competition broke when Captain Irving sold to Captain John T. Wright, Jr., and Captain Moore headed for Stikine River. Only Captains Millard and Wright were left on the Fraser. The two "had a meeting" and up went freight rates.

Captain Irving, though, wasn't leaving the river. He ordered a new vessel which was launched at Victoria on October 8. She was the *Reliance,* equipped with engines and other machinery salvaged from *Fort Yale.* But unlike the unfortunate latter vessel, *Reliance* was to sail long and profitably.

During 1862 occurred an incident which indicated that skippers had to contend not only with ruthless competition but also at times with unruly passengers. In June while the *Henrietta* was in Port Douglas about 90 miners came aboard and refused to pay their $5 fare or help work off the passage. The captain was a timid fellow and after seeking the advice of a justice of the peace who must have been equally timid, left for New Westminster. On the way down he met the *Hope* which belonged to the same line and pulled alongside. The result was described by a passenger on the *Henrietta:* "Captain Millard with several of his crew stepped aboard . . . and on hearing the facts of the case, immediately went around and collected the fare of $5 each from 80 or 90 men who, a few minutes before, were chuckling at the idea of having frightened the . . . captain of the *Henrietta* into giving them a free passage. It was rather amusing to see the very men who were 'broke' not five minutes before, coming down with their fares. . . . Those who really had no money

were taken back to Douglas . . . not because Captain Millard was too mean to bring them down, but because he wanted to teach them a lesson. . . ."

Some of the miners later complained of their treatment and Captain Millard answered in a letter to the *Victoria Colonist:* "I'm ready to swear neither knives nor pistols were used, and I did not consider there was any cause to fear. What I did I would do again under the same circumstances. When I am afraid to collect the fare from my passengers I will sail out and leave the country. It is an erroneous idea for men to think of taking steamboats and forcing their owners to do as they desire. It is true, steamboating on Fraser River is and has been one continued opposition, consequently the owners of them are looked upon as being fools. However, I have managed to run an independent boat, and have kept freights and passages at moderate figures; still I do not choose to have the boats run entirely for glory. If men travel with me they must pay, or give a good reason for not doing so."

The wreck of the ill-fated sidewheeler Cariboo *was purchased by McDougal Bros. and rebuilt. With a new but somewhat odd name of Cariboo and Fly she sailed the coast for many years.*
The Alexandra, *which Captain Moore intended to be the most lavish vessel on the coast. She was one of the few patterned after the twin-funnelled Mississippi River style of vessel, and was "by far the largest sternwheel boat on the northern coast, and when completed as the owners propose will also be the handsomest and most commodious." She was never completely finished because her owner went bankrupt. Her later career was also unsuccessful.*

When navigation opened in 1863, a stream of gold flowed southward, much of it over the nearly completed Cariboo Wagon Road. Downstream, sternwheelers carried bullion and miners, upstream they brought horses and oxen, stagecoaches and freight wagons, men and supplies. Advertisements in Victoria newspapers indicated variety of goods shipped to the goldfield. Clothing included lambswool undershirts, gumboots, drawers of all descriptions, Welsh flannel shirts, and oilskin trousers. There were guns, pistols, hatchets, frying pans, blacksmith's hardware, horse and mule shoes, sheet iron, and galvanized buckets. Blankets were listed, as was coconut matting, hearth rugs, newspapers and magazines, crockery, hanging wall lamps with silverized reflectors, window glass, dried fruits, English cheese, Scotch oatmeal, and Worcestershire sauce. Liquor was well represented with French, Spanish and American brandies; Jamaica rum in bulk; Scotch and Irish whisky in bulk or case; port, sherry, cider, clarets; and champagnes in various brands, in addition to a variety of gins and wines.

But as happened in 1862, a rate war started. United to fight Irving were Captain William Moore, who had returned from the Stikine, and John T. Wright. They proved no match for Captain Irving and his *Reliance*. The battle ended with Wright having to sell his vessels, among them the pioneer *Governor Douglas* and *Colonel Moody*. They were eventually taken to Puget Sound and broken up. The always optimistic Captain Moore then teamed up with Captain A. Insley. Moore was still flush with Stikine River profits where he had charged $100 a ton freight and made passengers cut firewood. He announced plans for a lavish $50,000 sternwheeler.

Meanwhile, three others appeared. Two of them, the *Seaton* and *Prince of Wales* were for use on the Harrison-Lillooet route, but their days were short. That year the wagon road through the Fraser Canyon was completed by the Royal Engineers and private contractors and Yale became portal to

Cariboo. The Harrison route with its many portages soon reverted to wilderness.

The third vessel to appear in 1863 was the *Lillooet*, built for Captain J. R. Fleming. At her launching the *Victoria Colonist* noted: "The flying sternwheel steamer . . . left the ways in gallant style. . . ." On the river she soon wore a set of antlers on her pilothouse, traditional symbol of speed queen. Unluckily for Captain Fleming, time was near when speed alone was no guarantee of solvency.

In early spring of 1864 another rate war broke out. Main participants were Captain Fleming and his *Lillooet*; Captain Millard with *Hope* and *Henrietta*; Irving with his *Reliance*; and the team of Moore and Insley. In command of Captain Moore's first sternwheeler, *Flying Dutchman*, was Jack Deighton, soon to establish a hotel and saloon on Burrard Inlet, first buildings in a community one day to be called Vancouver.

In May, additional competition appeared with completion of Moore's new vessel, the *Alexandra*. She was built like a Mississippi River sternwheeler, with twin funnels and was, according to one newspaper ". . . . by far the largest sternwheel boat on the northern coast, and when completed as the owners propose will also be the handsomest and most commodious. . . ." Her engines, "of the most powerful and elegant description," could drive her at 20 knots, but Moore learned also that speed itself wasn't profitable. Required were passengers and freight. Since Captain Irving had most of both, he won out.

Captain Fleming's *Lillooet* was sold to pay creditors as was Millard's *Hope*. Captain Moore took the *Alexandra* off the river but eventually lost her to creditors. Though the Captain was bankrupt, his B.C. sternwheel days were far from ended. His current misfortune, however, was a preview of economic conditions soon prevalent throughout British Columbia and Vancouver Island.

Lower Fraser River

PART TWO

At first wealth from the gravel of Cariboo seemed inexhaustible, but by 1865 the golden flow passed its crest. Although mines still yielded nuggets by the bucketful, winning them was increasingly difficult. Machinery replaced shovel and sluice box; wage earners substituted for free-spending miners of discovery claims. Traffic decreased, roadhouses closed, Victoria and New Westminster languished. On Fraser River, paddlewheelers reflected the times.

The *Caledonia* was dismantled by shipbuilder James Trahey to recover an unpaid-for boiler; *Flying Dutchman* and *Henrietta* were taken from service; Captain Moore's $50,000 *Alexandra* was sold at auction for $8,000. On the Harrison-Lillooet route, machinery from the *Champion* became a flour mill, while that from *Prince of Wales* was packed by mules over 200 miles northward to Cariboo. The only optimistic steam-boatman was Captain Irving. In 1865 he launched the *Onward,* but she was only a pinhole in a cloud of gloom.

Gold has proved a deceiving prop on which to base an economy. It caused inflation, attracted promoters, speculators, and similar unstable elements, and blinded men to other opportunities. In 1866 alone the colonies of British Columbia and Vancouver Island imported $500,000 of farm products, including California hay at $100 a ton, yet most of it could be grown locally. In 1864 a 150-acre field near Chilliwack yielded three tons an acre. As the *Victoria Colonist* noted: ". . . by digging no deeper than six inches from the surface the farmer may realize as handsome a return as the miner who delves in the creeks of Cariboo."

Soon only four sternwheelers plied the Fraser: *Onward* and *Reliance* operated by Captain Irving, and *Lillooet* and *Hope* by Captain Fleming. There was a flurry when gold was discovered in a region of Columbia River called the "Big Bend" but the area was greatly overrated and became known as the "Big Bilk."

By now both colonies were bankrupt. To consolidate administrative expenses, the British Government steered them into union. On November 19, 1866, they became the Crown

The Skuzzy in the Fraser Canyon in 1883. She plied the Canyon for two years, saving the railway contractors $10 a ton in road tolls alone.

Colony of British Columbia. But unification proved no stimulus to the economy. Captains Irving and Fleming "had a meeting" and agreed to run their vessels on alternate years and share profits.

In 1869 discovery of gold-bearing creeks in Omineca some 250 miles northwest of Quesnel generated a wave of optimism. Among those freighting to the area, this time with barges and mules, was Captain William Moore. Again the creeks were overrated. They reached a peak in 1871, then rapidly declined.

By 1871, however, occurred an event which was profoundly to affect the sternwheelers—British Columbia became a province in the Dominion of Canada, and terms of Union included a railway to be built to the Pacific Coast. In forthcoming years this railway would stoke sternwheelers to activity equalling the spectacular days of the gold rush, but by then many familiar skippers had sailed their last voyage. Among them were Captains Fleming, Wright, Parsons, Deighton and Irving.

The latter died suddenly at New Westminster on August 28, 1872. In the community flags were flown at half mast, and the local paper commented: ". . . the sad news of the death of this gentleman . . . fell like a pall on the entire community. His name will be held in respect by British Columbians as long as one of the present generation exists."

Irving's 18-year-old son, John, took over his father's business. Although young he was every ounce a riverboatman, able to drink and fight with the best. In 1873 at 19 he took command of the *Onward*, and after his first trip to Yale the *New Westminster Mainland Guardian* commented: "Great praise is awarded to Capt. Irving for the able way in which

The second Reliance *at Yale. When she was launched in March 1876, the* Victoria Colonist *reported: ". . . the steamer, without a jar—without a single tremor, started into life, and like the flight of a seagull, floated out upon the waters of Rock Bay." Her career on the Fraser was as successful as her launching.*

he handled the boat in going up and returning. The settlers on the way, up and down, cheered the steamer. . . ."

Next year he experienced his first rate war. Yet another gold rush was on, this time to northwestern B.C. in the mountainous Cassiar country. Captain Moore was again involved; he had, in fact, led the way and in 1873 with his three sons staked Discovery Claim on Dease Creek. Since reports from the area were favorable, John Irving ordered a new sternwheeler, the *Glenora.* She was launched March 9, 1874, and next month headed for Stikine River, portal to the new goldfield.

Captain Parsons also went north with his *Hope,* but competition was brief. In June, the two captains "had a meeting." As a consequence, Irving returned to the Fraser but shared profits earned by the *Hope.*

Captain Moore, for once, wasn't involved in competition. He had a government charter authorizing him to build a pack trail from Stikine River to the creeks and charge two cents a pound toll for freight plus .50 cents a head for horses and cattle. Since some 5,000 men were in the region, he prospered. Eventually, he and his sons earned some $100,000 from their claims and pack trail. Unfortunately, Captain Moore far preferred a sternwheeler's helm to a horse's halter, and was destined to lose every cent.

He returned to Victoria and ordered a new sternwheeler. She was the *Gertrude,* launched on March 22, 1875. She had 10 watertight compartments, timbers from yellow cedar brought from Fort Simpson, and everything in "the lightest and most substantial manner possible." With her Moore returned in triumph to the Stikine.

Meanwhile there had appeared on Burrard Inlet a paddlewheeler of remarkable simplicity. She was the *Union,* a cooperative arrangement between two men, one of whom had a scow; the other, a threshing machine engine. They married this combination, attached name and paddlewheels, and looked for customers. The novel craft served for years, despite a few quirks. She didn't have steam pressure enough to operate whistle and paddlewheel simultaneously; consequently the skipper had to be cautious with the whistle lanyard— when he pulled it the paddlewheels stopped. She had no reverse gear and had to drift into dock. This lack of reverse made fast stops a problem, but in emergencies a sack was tossed into the gears, bringing her up with a "sudden jerk." Since she started her tow by taking a run at it, she also got underway with a "sudden jerk." With these traits, it wasn't surprising that she was known not as *Union,* but as *Sudden Jerk.*

On the Fraser in 1875 the season was quiet. A new vessel,

the *Royal City,* had appeared, built by Captain Parsons as opposition to Irving. A newspaper said she was "the finest specimen of steamboat work yet turned out in the province" but Parsons didn't operate her long. In June he retired, selling her to Captain Irving. That November with his wife and daughter he sailed for California on the steamer *Pacific.* A few hours after the vessel left Victoria she collided with the *Orpheus* near Cape Flattery and sank. Of over 250 people on board, only two survived. Among those drowned were Captain Parsons and his family.

The *Pacific* tragedy overshadowed another rate war on the Fraser. Captain Moore arrived from Stikine and challenged Irving. Fares dropped to $1 from New Westminster to Yale and freight to $2 a ton. Moore found Irving just as capable as his father and after a few weeks headed back north.

Irving, however, decided to challenge Moore and ordered a new vessel especially designed for Stikine River. She was the *Reliance,* launched at Victoria on March 7, 1876. Moore knew that she would be tough competition. He "had a meet-

At upper right is Captain Irving's house, built in 1862-64. The house was bought by the city of New Westminster in 1950 and is now an historic center.
At right is G. B. Wright who built much of the Cariboo Wagon Road and was part owner of the Enterprise.
Captain Asbury Insley, far right, arrived on the Fraser in 1858 and was active for over 40 years. At times he was Captain Moore's partner, at times his rival; at other times he commanded his own vessel, and when broke worked for wages. Like most pioneer skippers he was American, but remained in B.C. and contributed greatly to development of the province.

ing" with Irving, and the *Reliance* thereafter stayed on the Fraser and Moore on the Stikine.

But to Moore the Fraser was an irresistible siren and next season he again ventured south. This time Irving had additional competition from his own former vessel, the *Glenora*, which Captain Moore chartered to Yale businessmen. Fares to Yale dropped to .25 cents, freight to .50 cents a ton. *Glenora* even carried passengers direct from Victoria to Yale for .50 cents, including meals and bed. The public was delighted. Crowds gathered at Yale and New Westminster to welcome the boats, with Irving hiring a band to "discourse sweet music at intervals along the route." Competition was too ruthless to last, and Captain Moore again headed back to Stikine. Later, Irving bought the *Glenora* and once more monopolized river traffic.

Peace on the river, however, wasn't reflected in either Victoria or New Westminster. The two were fighting over which was to be western terminus of the trans-continental railway the Dominion Government agreed to build when B.C. became a province. New Westminster favored a route down the Fraser Canyon; Victoria argued that the best way was via the Chilcotin to Bute Inlet, then across Seymour Narrows to Vancouver Island. The Liberal government felt otherwise. In July, 1878, they chose the Canyon route.

Irving won a contract to transport 5,000 tons of steel rails to Yale. When the *Royal City* arrived with her first cargo, she was met by a 21-gun salute, fluttering flags, and a "grand display of fireworks." New Westminster gloated, certain that they had outdone Victoria

But their triumph was fleeting. Next election Liberals were ousted and the incoming Conservatives cancelled all contracts. Now Victoria smiled. But on October 4, 1879 their bubble of optimism burst when the Conservatives also chose the Canyon route.

One man unconcerned about the railway fuss was Captain William Moore. He was still on the Stikine, and had even built a new sternwheeler, the *Western Slope*. But the Captain, as persistent as autumn frost, would again return to the

The Yosemite was originally constructed for the Sacramento River trade in California. In October 1865 she blew up, killing 55 people. She was repaired and with a 35-foot splice in her hull and new boilers went back into service. In 1883 Captain John Irving bought her and put her on the Victoria-New Westminster then the Victoria-Vancouver run. She served for 22 years, then in 1905 returned to the U.S. In August 1907 she rammed through 30 feet of Seattle's dock area, knocking over a surprised horse and wagon. She thus became the first—and only—paddlewheeler to collide with a horse—and a harnessed horse, at that.

The William Irving at Yale about 1881. Like many seamen, her owner, Captain John Irving, was superstitious. He felt it unlucky to carry a gray horse and a parson. At Chilliwack Landing he once refused to let a parson on board. The parson objected, first with dignity, then with increasing warmth and decreasing dignity. Irving remained firm. He had carried the combination of a gray horse and a parson three times he pointed out, and each time met with a mishap. He already had a gray horse aboard and wasn't adding a parson. The boat churned away with the parson still angrily arguing on the wharf.

Fraser—with the inevitable uproar and disaster to himself.

In 1879 Captain Irving experienced his first steamboat loss when *Glenora* snagged herself above Harrison River and sank. To replace her and meet the competition railway construction would bring, he ordered a new vessel, the *William Irving.*

By 1881, 5,000 men were at work on a 29-mile section of railway between Emory and Boston Bar alone, and all came upriver on sternwheelers. So did supplies, machinery and construction material, with the bridge across Fraser River at Cisco alone requiring 6,000 tons of steel. Five sternwheelers were on the river: John Irving's *Reliance, Royal City,* and *William Irving;* while Captain Moore, who had again returned to the Fraser, ran the *Cassiar* and *Western Slope.* It was a combination guaranteed to erupt.

First indication that things were simmering was a seemingly innocent news item in the *Victoria Colonist* that "Captain Moore was served with a summons at New Westminster for putting a drunken Indian off the boat recently."

The New Westminster paper reported that: "The man was neither drunk nor an Indian, but a respectable Englishman and a duly certified engineer, who says he left Captain Moore's employment for good and sufficient reasons which are likely to come before the public very soon. . . ."

Further details appeared June 15 with the announcement that Captain Moore had been summoned to appear before Magistrate's Court in New Westminster to answer a charge of carrying greater steam pressure than the law allowed. The case aroused immediate interest, and the story that unfurled re-affirmed the belief among veteran sternwheel passengers that a fatalistic attitude was a good travelling companion.

The *Western Slope* was equipped with a steam gauge to reassure passengers. Evidence indicated, however, that it registered 40 pounds low. In addition, one safety valve was wedged shut and couldn't release without first blowing the floor out of the cabin above. The other safety valve, reported a fireman, hadn't blown even with 40 per cent more pressure

than the law permitted. Captain Moore and his engineer were fined $200 each for carrying excessive steam.

Apart from this minor inconvenience, the season was profitable for Moore. The New Westminster paper later noted: "The steamer *Western Slope* has certainly enjoyed a remarkable run of success during the greater part of this season, coming and going with a degree of regularity that shames some other boats, and sailing through Dominion statutes with as much assurance as she would run over a luckless fisherman's net."

Captain Irving was also in the news. At Victoria on June 18 he launched the *Elizabeth J. Irving*, first sternwheeler equipped with a new feature known as "electric lights." She had 25 watertight compartments so that "being snagged in several of them at the same time will not materially interfere with her progress," and laden to capacity with 350 tons of freight, required only three feet of water. Said the *Victoria Colonist* at her launching: "We congratulate the country upon this splendid addition to its steam marine and hope

that the *Elizabeth J. Irving* may long survive to annihilate time and distance between the head and foot of Inland Navigation of the province."

Unfortunately, she didn't long survive. On her second voyage she caught fire at Hope. The $50,000 vessel together with $60,000 in cargo was soon a smoking hulk, a funeral pyre for four Indians, two horses, and two cows. For Irving, the loss was harsh, especially since a $50,000 insurance policy ex-

---

Hope as it looked when the gold rush waned. At bottom is Vancouver in 1884. The first building appeared in 1867 when a sternwheel captain, John Deighton, opened a shake-roofed saloon. Since Captain Deighton was somewhat talkative, the community which grew around his saloon was named Gastown in his honor. Later the name was changed to Granville, then in 1884 to Vancouver. When Captain Deighton died in 1875 at 45, a newspaper noted that he "was an original in his way, and his name became almost a household word with most of our citizens."

pired a week previously. But with characteristic courage he salvaged what he could and ordered an even larger vessel.

At the beginning of the next season, another sternwheeler was wrecked. She was the *Cassiar*, which on April 12 on her first trip crunched into rocks three miles above Hope and sank. During high water two months later she was washed free, caught in a whirlpool, and tossed bottom up in front of the *Pacific Slope*. Only alertness by Captain H. Moore, William Moore's son, prevented the wreck from ramming his vessel. The *Cassiar's* pilothouse eventually floated downstream to a slough near Harrison River where it was salvaged and used by a farmer as a chicken coop.

On June 10 Captain Irving's new sternwheeler, *R. P. Rithet*, arrived at New Westminster on her maiden voyage, her electric lights "shining with dazzling brilliancy and the New Westminster Militia Band playing a lively air." She was the finest vessel yet to appear. The New Westminster paper reported: "Perfect in lines and model, she is finished and found in every respect in first class style. The carving in the saloons is elaborate and ornate, while the upholstering, gilding and general finish are simply gorgeous. In short, in the perfection of her lines, the completeness of her appointments, and the elegance of design and finish, the *R. P. Rithet* is truly a floating palace." In contrast to the unfortunate *E. J. Irving*, she was to sail long and profitably.

Another sternwheeler which appeared in 1882 was the *Skuzzy*, launched May 4 at Spuzzum in the formidable gorge of Fraser Canyon. Her owner was railway contractor Andrew Onderdonk who intended to "sail the *Skuzzy* upriver through Hells Gate to Boston Bar and transport supplies by boat from Lytton to Boston Bar." Many veteran steamboatmen said the feat was impossible. Others weren't sure, pointing out that Onderdonk wasn't an ordinary man. Before he was 30 he

---

The R. P. Rithet on the Fraser River in 1887. Places where the vessels called along the river were known as "Landings," usually named after a pioneer resident—Wade, Miller, Lehman, Nicholson, and dozens more.

had over 5,000 men working on $10,000,000 worth of railway construction through the Fraser and Thompson Canyons.

The challenge facing *Skuzzy* was awesome. She would have to beat through a rock-walled cleft so narrow that the river got off its belly and slid through sideways, where speed of the current far exceeded that of the *Skuzzy,* and where fluctuation between low and high water could exceed 100 feet.

First skipper hired was Captain Nat Lane, Jr., a whitewater man with experience on the Willamette, Fraser, and Stikine Rivers. Lane looked at the rock-ripped, boiling waterway and promptly left. Veteran Ausbury Insley replaced him and on May 17 swung *Skuzzy* into the current.

She worked her way through gorges whose rock walls with their crown of evergreens turned daylight to dusk; whose sheer volume of water threatened to sweep her downstream; and whose crosscurrents and whirlpools swept her towards one wall then the other. But Captain Insley was a seafarer of 30 years. He gradually worked the *Skuzzy* upstream, under

the Royal Engineers' famous suspension bridge, through Black Canyon, then to the constriction called Hell's Gate. She stuck her nose into the entrance and was bashed by rapids where water tumbled through at 25 feet a second, where shouted commands were inaudible above the pulsating roar.

As *Skuzzy* strained to force a passage, spray from her bow squirted mast high, while black smoke and white steam hurried skyward, eager to escape the battle below. With whirling paddlewheel beating the brown water white and steam pipes crackling under forced pressure, she again and again shuddered into the waves of water foaming through the rock constriction. But the struggle was futile. The rapids, their power magnified by the highest water in 40 years, were impassable.

By now, only Onderdonk believed she could reach Boston Bar without being dismantled and freighted overland. He sent to Oregon for Captain S. R. Smith and his brother, David. On September 7 when the river had dropped, *Skuzzy* swung once more into the silt-laden current. At Hell's Gate

progress again stopped. For ten days she assaulted the rapids but each attempt failed. Onderdonk ordered ringbolts drilled into the rock walls, then stationed 125 Chinese along the rim. Finally, with Chinese tugging on a tow rope, steam capstan inching in cable, safety valve popping, and paddlewheel throbbing, *Skuzzy* inched up the rapids and won the crest. She arrived at Boston Bar soon after, 16 days to beat 16 miles from Spuzzum, but 16 of the most turbulent miles any sternwheeler faced. The *Inland Sentinel* commented, in an understatement: "We must say that Capt. Smith and his assistants got the Railway Company out of . . . a difficulty."

While *Skuzzy* was making history in the Canyon, sternwheelers on the Lower Fraser were again in ruthless competition. As could be expected, Captain Moore was involved, but Irving once more steamed over his opposition. The season ended with Moore's creditors seizing his sternwheelers, house, and other assets. But bankruptcy was only a temporary obstacle to Moore. He had bounced back in the past; he would in the future.

Captain William Moore, upper right, was the most colorful of all B.C.'s sternwheeler skippers. He took part in every B.C. gold rush, including the Queen Charlottes in 1852, Fraser in 1858, Stikine in 1862, Big Bend in 1865, then Omineca, Cassiar, and Klondike. Wherever gold was found, Moore would arrive with supplies, by sailing barge, pack mule, or sternwheeler. He pioneered navigation on the Stikine where hazards included hostile Indians who told him to leave since his paddlewheeler was scaring the fish. Moore was not easily intimidated and remained, although Indians later killed his son. Moore died in Victoria on March 30, 1909 at 87, a bold and adventuresome pioneer. Andrew Onderdonk, upper left, built the Skuzzy and the formidable Fraser Canyon section of the C.P.R. After the Skuzzy had been defeated by Hells Gate, opposite, only Onderdonk had faith in her.

The William Irving at Emory Bar downstream from Yale. When light she could sail in fifteen inches of water, when loaded with 300 tons of freight required only three feet. She cost $75,000 and had sleeping accommodation for 55 passengers in berths which "are all fitted with patent spring mattresses" and of "comfortable dimensions."

During the next four years, however, occurred two developments which virtually ended the rousing days of individual skippers. The Canadian Pacific Navigation Company was formed, with 29-year-old Captain Irving general manager. Vessels which the $500,000 company didn't own it bought, making monopoly backed by large capital at last a reality. Then completion of the C.P.R. in 1886 changed a transportation pattern established during the gold rush nearly 20 years before. Replacing Yale as portal to Cariboo was a new community called Ashcroft; much of Fraser Valley was now supplied by rail instead of sternwheeler, and a new city called Vancouver ended the fighting for supremacy between Victoria and New Westminster. Sternwheelers still served communities on the south bank of the Fraser and new vessels did appear, but generally they were built by companies for their own use or intended for local trade.

One of the latter class was the *Adelaide*, first of a series to serve canneries and communities springing up along the river. Although the smaller vessels weren't as glamorous as their elaborate sisters, they lacked none of the color, as the following item from *New Westminster British Columbian* reveals: "The steam(er) *Adelaide* passed up at full speed on Thursday morning, her decks crowded with Indians beating empty oil cans and dancing something very like a war-dance, having in tow two large scows and a flotilla of Indian canoes, and having specimens of the sockeye tribe suspended from the top of poles."

Several sternwheelers participated in rescue work in June 1894 when the Fraser River reached a record flood level, isolating hundreds of settlers. The *Gladys, Courser,* and *Transfer* sailed far inland from the main channel of the river, casually crossing gardens and fences and tieing up to barns and houses. The *Transfer* sailed over what had been Nicomen Island and loaded 100 stranded cattle, while the *Courser* steamed across the garden in front of one home and picked up boxes of fowl from the front verandah. At another place a settler boarded the rescue vessel from the upper window of his house. After one salvage trip the *Inland Sentinel* re-

ported that the *Courser* was loaded with "cattle and settler's effects, plus seven dogs of various sizes and a barrel of bears."

The last flurry on the Lower Fraser was stirred by the stampede to Klondike. In October 1897, Federal government officials announced plans for an all-Canadian route to Yukon. It would be up Stikine River to Telegraph Creek from where a 150-mile-long railway would connect to Teslin Lake, thence by sternwheeler to Dawson City.

Several companies started building sternwheelers to serve

The Delaware, bow nosed into the bank of the Fraser River, demonstrates the versatility of sternwheelers. Passengers and livestock came aboard over a short gangplank.

The Western Slope, bottom right, is the vessel which Captain Moore operated with one safety valve set to read low and the other jammed shut with a block of wood.

The Gladys, below, is believed by some to have caused the fire which wiped out downtown New Westminster in 1898.

the route, the C.P.R. alone planning a fleet of 20. Unfortunately, the projected all-Canadian route collapsed when politics killed the railway plan. By then, many new sternwheelers were ready, including *Victorian, Columbian, Canadian, Monte Cristo, Iskoot, Stikine, Hamlin,* and *Ogilvie.*

On May 15, 1898, the *Victoria Colonist* reported that seven sternwheelers had already left for the north and 12 days later noted that a fleet of five would sail that day alone. But without the railway as a stimulus, the Stikine route quickly reverted to wilderness. Of all sternwheelers built, only two would have useful careers. They were *Moyie* and *Minto,* built in eastern Canada but diverted to Kootenay and Arrow Lakes when the Stikine route collapsed.

Oddly enough, one person not involved in the Stikine excitement was Captain William Moore, even though he had pioneered the river almost a half century before. The Captain was once again settled ashore—and prospering.

After going bankrupt on the Fraser in 1882, he headed north. Once he worked with a boundary survey party, and

with an Indian named Skookum Jim—later to be a co-discoverer of Klondike—explored a route into Yukon from tidewater at the head of Lynn Canal. Famed Canadian surveyor William Ogilvie named the route "White Pass." Moore was convinced that one day a major gold strike would be made in Yukon, and in 1891 tried unsuccessfully to get permission from the U.S. Government to build a toll road over White Pass. In 1895 he guided a party of miners to Yukon by a new route soon to be a symbol of hardship—Chilkoot Pass. Next year he won a mail contract from the Canadian Government. Although 74, he travelled by foot and dogteam hundreds of wilderness miles throughout Yukon, carrying mail for isolated miners searching the creeks. When the big strike was finally made on Bonanza, Moore was around to stake a claim. It was later jumped, and all he received was $1,000.

The old veteran, however, was growing rich. He had been so sure that Yukon would yield treasure that in 1888 he built a cabin and a wharf at the head of Lynn Canal and applied for 60 acres of land. When the Klondike rush started nearly a decade later, White and Chilkoot Passes became main entry point for the goldfield. Men by the boatload and supplies by thousands of tons passed over Moore's wharf, while on his land grew the community of Skagway.

While Captain Moore prospered, sternwheelers on Lower Fraser sailed into twilight. On September 10, 1898, the *Gladys, Edgar,* and *Bon Accord* burned in the fire which swept through 60 blocks of downtown New Westminster. Cause of the $2,500,000 blaze was never determined. Some people felt it was started deliberately, some said a spark

---

Most sternwheelers for Fraser-Stikine Rivers were built at Vancouver and Victoria, with the capital city in particular building many vessels. Among them was the Port Simpson launched in 1908. She had her trial trip April 20, with the Victoria Colonist reporting: "Everything went beautifully. Officers in new uniforms hurried hither and thither as the ship slowly steamed out of port, while the passengers gathered in the handsomely furnished saloon. . . ."

from a passing sternwheeler was responsible, others insisted it started on the *Gladys*. Whatever the cause, the fire devastated 100 acres of New Westminster and wiped out many landmarks familiar to pioneer river travellers.

In January, 1901, another pioneer link severed. The C.P.R. bought the Canadian Pacific Navigation Company's entire fleet. Terms of sale provided that Captain John Irving could travel free on C.P.R. vessels, a clause that became most important to Irving. While fate was kind to William Moore in his old age, it was the opposite with Irving.

Sale of the fleet hastened replacement of paddlewheel by propellor. Gone were rousing decades of independent skippers, jammed safety valves, and free rides with brass bands. But, as could be expected, the sternwheelers refused to leave peacefully.

At Mission on April 10, 1901, the *Royal City* burned, killing two deckhands. A week later the *Ramona* blew up while approaching Morrison's Landing near Fort Langley, killing four people. One victim was Mrs. Morrison whose waiting husband witnessed the tragedy.

The *Ramona* was originally built to serve on Stikine River during the Klondike rush. On the Fraser she ran in opposition to the *Transfer*, the pair staging many races. Since the *Transfer* usually proved the faster, *Ramona's* owners installed a bigger boiler. It was the one which exploded.

Despite the explosion, *Ramona's* days were not yet over. On July 16 with a new boiler "staunch as could be desired," she resumed regular trips. Twilight, although darkening, had not yet enveloped the sternwheelers.

In December 1904 the *New Westminster Daily Columbian* reported that "several steamers of large capacity and excellently fitted for passenger traffic, afford means of travelling to the valley of the Fraser, from the coast to Chilliwack and Harrison. The steamer *Transfer* runs from New Westminster to Ladner and Steveston, and connects the other places of call along the river. Daily service is kept up each way, winter and summer. On the upper river there are 4 steamers. The *Beaver*, which like the *Transfer* is owned and operated by

The Paystreak at Yale. In the latter days of sternwheelers, Hamlin and Ramona ran in competition. Charles Warner, one of Hamlin's crew, recalled that they got the elderly passengers while Ramona got the young folk because she had a bar. At the time Chilliwack had prohibition and a notable item of cargo was jugs of vinegar. "In fact," stated Mr. Warner, "so many jugs were confined to the various business places in Chilliwack that I thought the community had a pickle factory."

The Beaver, upper right, launched at Victoria in 1898, was the first steel-hulled sternwheeler—and the first steel ship—built in the province. The Transfer, opposite, was among the last on the Fraser. Completion of the C.P.R. didn't immediately displace sternwheelers. Many communities were still isolated and between New Westminster and Chilliwack there were some 30 regular calls, plus many others wherever a white flag flew. Upriver trip took about nine hours; return, about seven, depending on the number of calls.

Captain William Irving, far left, was the most popular and successful of all gold-rush skippers, and always emerged victorious from the ruthless rate wars. He was the first president of New Westminster city council and when he died the Mainland Guardian edged its advertisements and news columns with black in tribute.

John Irving, left, took over his father's business in 1872 when only 18. He was active on both the Lower and Upper Fraser River, the Thompson-Shuswap system, and Columbia and Yukon Rivers. Oddly, as the sternwheel era closed, his fortunes declined. When C.P.R. bought his company, a clause stated that he could ride C.P.R. vessels free. In later years Captain Irving was almost broke and travelled constantly on C.P.R. ships, which became a home to him. Marine historian Norman Hacking describes him as: "Well over 6 feet in height . . . a two-fisted fighter, a great social favourite, a mighty drinker, and the soul of generosity. He overcame all rivals, built up a great business empire, was a member of the Provincial Legislature for many years, and died in Vancouver in 1936, poor in everything but friends."

This advertisement is reproduced from the Victoria Colonist of April 20, 1880 when Captains Moore and Irving were in one of their frequent rate wars. Since Moore ran a through service from Victoria to Yale, he extolled the virtues of not having to stop overnight at New Westminster with "heavy expense for hotel accommodation, etc." Irving, on the other hand, pointed out that passengers on any line but his spent the night in "the midst of an impenetrable forest. . . ." Opposite: Skeena, as she ended her days on the Fraser.

the C.P.R. is run to Chilliwack, alternating with the steamer Ramona owned by a local company. These steamers give the river valley settlers a regular service all the year around, being seldom interrupted, and that only for a few days in mid-winter occasionally by ice which sometimes jams in the river. The steamers Favourite and Defender are run from New Westminster up the river to Mount Lehman, Mission and other points. Once a year the steamer Beaver makes a trip up Harrison River and Lake with supplies to Fort Douglas, the Hudson's Bay post at the head of Harrison Lake."

For several more years sternwheelers continued to serve Valley residents. Then in 1907, twilight started turning to darkness. Construction started on a $3,500,000 electric railway to link New Westminster and Chilliwack. It was completed October 3, 1910 and offered speed and convenience sternwheelers couldn't match.

In 1909 Ramona sank near Harrison River and was abandoned. The Transfer went to Redonda Bay and became a power plant for a cannery. A new vessel to appear was the Paystreak. Her career was brief, although she did become the last sternwheeler to call at Yale. The remaining vessels sailed into the night until only one was left.

She was the Skeena, built in 1908 to help construct the Grand Trunk Pacific Railway along the Skeena River. When the line was completed her usefulness was over. In 1914 she was purchased by Captain Charles E. Seymour to serve on the Fraser. For 11 years she plied the river, becoming a familiar landmark. "As she sails, week after week, past the low shores of Surrey, Langley and Matsqui, of Coquitlam, Pitt Meadows, Maple Ridge and Mission, she seems to carry some of that nearly dead romance of the river," noted the Vancouver Province. "Even when crowded with holiday makers . . . she wears still that air of simple dignity particular to the pioneer. Much has she done toward building up of the valley. Long may she continue."

As long as Captain Seymour lived, she did continue and a link remained with the spirited days of the 1858 Fraser River gold rush. Then in 1925 Captain Seymour died and the Skeena was tied up at New Westminster. The local Board of Trade tried to find a way of putting her back in operation, but were unsuccessful. Finally, she was auctioned to Ewan's Cannery for $5,000 and converted into a floating boarding house. Later, her hull was used as a barge by an oil company.

Thus closed an era born 67 years before. During this period Indian trails and trappers' paths became a network of roads and railways; the flamboyant community of Victoria matured into a stately capital; a brash newcomer, Vancouver, grew into a major city; and an unexplored wilderness was becoming Canada's third wealthiest province. It was an amazing transformation, and in it sternwheelers and their crews had been prominent and vital.

F
and
Oct
in (
the
led
the
Ne(
tor
fina
whi
pro
Ii
incl
pas
Sen
yor
"ha
rap

Op
lef
Fo
Ab
to

CHAPTER FOUR

Cariboo and Central B.C.

From her birthplace at Cowdung Lake on the western slopes of the Rocky Mountains to Soda Creek in the Cariboo, the Fraser River flows 500 miles, about one-half of her total journey to tidewater. Much of the route she is placid, but in several areas she punches through rock barriers, leaving in her wake rock-toothed canyons that acquired a mean reputation from their very first exploration by Alexander Mackenzie and Simon Fraser. One is a mile long, another seven, but short and long had a common trait—they could disembowel a sternwheeler with the deftness of a surgeon's scalpel.

During various periods from 1863 to 1921, 12 paddlewheelers plied the Upper Fraser, providing a service from Soda Creek over 400 miles upstream to within sight of lofty Mt. Robson. Some vessels were powerful and ornate; others, less pretentious. Among the latter was one built at Fort George in 1910 by real estate promoter, Billy Davis.

"I never saw Billy's boat, but heard of her," wrote Wiggs O'Neill, well-known pioneer resident. "She was built like a scow, with a shovel nose. Her stern was square, as if she were made by the yard, then sawn off, took what was required and left the rest. She had a big stationary gas engine and a paddlewheel run by chains, an awful contraption that couldn't get out of her own way. Billy apparently intended naming her *W. E. Davis* after himself, but was so disgusted with his creation he took off, leaving his vessel unnamed and unmourned."

The pioneer vessel on the Upper Fraser River appeared during the Cariboo gold rush. She was the *Enterprise*, built near Fort Alexandria, the area where in 1793 Alexander Mackenzie decided to abandon the river and continue by land his historic trek to the Pacific. She wasn't large, 110 feet long by 20 wide, but the fact that she appeared at all was a triumph. Every foot of lumber was hand sawn, with boiler, engines,

---

The B.X. at Fort George Landing in 1910. She was among the finest sternwheelers to sail inland waters. Her dining room could seat 50 and her staterooms had steam heat, reading lights, wash stand, fan, and were finished with red velvet carpeting and green curtains. Fully laden with passengers and 100 tons of freight she could work in water shallow enough for a man to wade.

the *Prince of Wales* on Lillooet Lake, they were serviceable and lasted until 1886 when the aging vessel was hauled ashore and left to decay near Fort Alexandria.

For a decade no smoke plume twirled above the cutbanks or shrill whistle pierced autumn mists that cloaked the river. Then on August 3, 1896 a new sternwheeler was launched at Quesnel. A correspondent for the *Ashcroft, B.C. Mining Journal* wrote: ". . . about 3:00 o'clock in the afternoon the S.S. *Charlotte* was launched into the chilling waters of the Fraser. . . . Everything went as merrily as a marriage bell. . . . As the cord was cut and the boat began to dart gallantly into the water Mrs. Senator Reid, after who the boat is named, christened her in royal style and according to the old-time custom by breaking a bottle of champagne against the bow." The paper also noted that after the event there were a "goodly number of corks for sale around town as souvenirs."

For 13 years the *Charlotte* plied the river alone, then in 1909 two new vessels joined her. Stimulus was the Grand Trunk Pacific Railway under construction 1,757 miles from Winnipeg through Central B.C. to the Pacific at a new port called Prince Rupert. The railway started a pulse beat in a land long dormant.

First of the new vessels was launched at Quesnel on May 29, 1909. She was the *Nechacco*, described as ". . . an ideal type of river boat. . . . Owing to her light draft, about thirteen inches, she will be able to go places in the Fraser and Nechako Rivers which have been impossible hitherto for the larger and heavier steamers." The prediction was later fulfilled when she pioneered nearly 400 miles of the Nechako and Fraser Rivers.

The second vessel was grandly called the *City of Quesnel*. Built for Telesphore Marion, pioneer Quesnel merchant and fur trader, by John Strand, a Quesnel carpenter, she was designed to burn local coal instead of wood. Her captain, D. A. Foster, was also a local man, making her a genuine hometown product. Unfortunately for local pride, she sat rather heavy in the water. She was hauled ashore, her hull lengthened and name shortened, and as *Quesnel* launched again on

Stagecoach on the Cariboo Road near Quesnel. Originally the journey from Yale to the sternwheel terminus at Soda Creek took 52 hours, but when Ashcroft became portal to Cariboo time was reduced to 42 hours. The stage left Ashcroft at 4 a.m. on Monday and Friday for the 167-mile journey and arrived at Soda Creek at 10 o'clock next night. At right the Charlotte pulls into Fort George in 1910. She made her first trip to the area in 1908, leading the Ashcroft Journal to comment: "The foregoing will be good news to all travellers going into the northern interior, as the trip will now be a comparative short and easy one. With the Cariboo Automobile Company making regular trips to Quesnel and Soda Creek and also the stageline it will now only be a matter of 4 or 5 days . . . to Fort George from Ashcroft."

September 2, probably the only sternwheeler to have two launchings in a year. She was never much of a success, but she was to be the last sternwheeler on the Upper Fraser.

In the spring of 1910, three additional vessels appeared. They were the *B.X.*, owned by the B.C. Express Company, a pioneer transportation firm; and the *Fort Fraser* and *Chilcotin*, built for a rival firm, the Fort George Lumber and Navigation Company. The *B.X.* was designed to carry over 100 tons of freight plus 130 passengers upstream on a twice-a-week schedule to Fort George, an objective generally considered impossible.

Since the *B.X.* and the *Chilcotin* were to operate competitively, there was intense rivalry between shipyard crews at Soda Creek. The *Chilcotin* supporters started a rumor that the *B.X.* was too wide to pass through the low-water channel of Fort George Canyon and would prove a white elephant. Thereafter the B.C. Express Company received letters from friends hoping that they wouldn't go bankrupt in venturing from stagecoach to steam.

The *B.X.* was launched on Friday, May 13 without champagne or ceremony of any kind. This breach of marine tradition was to the superstitious additional proof of impending disaster. Under command of Captain O. F. Browne she arrived at Quesnel on Victoria Day, and "with the flags of the empire and the company fore and aft she presented a spectacle never before seen upon the mighty Fraser in this northern interior." Before long she was known not as "White Elephant" but as "Queen of the North."

After a month plying between Quesnel and Soda Creek she headed upstream 93 miles to Fort George. Two major obstructions were Cottonwood Canyon, a mile-long series of rocks and rapids 18 miles above Quesnel, and Fort George Canyon, 15 miles south of Fort George. Here the river splits into three channels, and of it Alexander Mackenzie wrote in his diary: "The great body of water, at the same time tumbling in successive cascades . . . rolls through this narrow passage in a very turbid current, and full of whirlpools." In 1833 David Douglas, the famous Scots botanist after whom

the Douglas fir is named, nearly drowned in one of the whirl-pools. His canoe was swamped and he was swirled around for nearly two hours before being washed ashore. The Canyon was to reap a heavier toll of sternwheelers than any other in British Columbia.

On her maiden voyage Captain Browne safely piloted the B.X. through both canyons. He proceeded upstream until he saw people waiting to welcome him a short distance from the H.B.C. post of Fort George at the junction of the Fraser and Nechako Rivers. He nosed his vessel ashore and around the landing grew the flamboyant community of South Fort George. Meanwhile, three miles away on the bank of the Nechako River, another new community, Fort George, was being established by a promoter called G. J. Hammond. As the communities grew so did rivalry between them. Eventually each had a newspaper and the result was startling. The editor of the South Fort George paper considered Hammond a liar, among other things, and said so. On the other hand the editor of the Fort George paper was equally blunt, refer-ring to his counterpart as a "red-light agent" whose writings were the "ravings of a mangy idiot."

To promote his townsite, Hammond spent over $500,000 on a world-wide publicity campaign and sold over 12,000 lots to people buying mainly on speculation. On one map, Fort George was shown as being the hub of no less than 11 rail-ways, either chartered or building, while only one was pro-jected and that was many miles and four years away. A problem for Hammond was that South Fort George became the steamboat terminus and many people attracted north by his optimistic salesmanship were sold lots in South Fort George before they could reach Fort George. To counteract this advantage, Fort George salesmen rode upstream on the sternwheelers, giving rise to a story that one unfortunate speculator sailed over his property as he came upstream on the B.X.

In his book A History of Prince George, the Reverend F. E. Runnalls relates what happened when the purchaser saw his real estate and realized that he had been fleeced. As the fel-

The Nechacco fighting through a canyon on the Nechako River. In 1909-10 Captain J. H. Bonser pioneered two water-ways with her. The first took him up the Nechako and Nautely Rivers into Fraser Lake, 90 miles west of Fort George. On the second he ventured 315 miles up the Fraser River from Fort George to Tete Jaune Cache, only 53 miles from the Alberta border.

At right is the B.C. Express. Her captain, J. P. Bucey, was an outstanding whitewater skipper. He started as a boy on the Mississippi River, then sailed on the Columbia and Yukon, plus 14 seasons on the Skeena before coming to the Upper Fraser. He was the only skipper to maintain a regular schedule through the Upper Fraser River's awesome Grand Canyon, a torrent that claimed dozens of lives.

low sat on the bank of the Nechako River, looking glumly across to the cutbank on the other side, he was asked his problem.

"Do you see that sand bank over there?" he replied. "Well, I spent all I had on four lots in Bella Vista subdivision, right on the edge of that bank. Every time one of the slides comes down, I figure it costs me fifty dollars. I've lost two hundred dollars since nine o'clock this morning, and I don't know whether to jump in the river or go back East and sell the lots to my brother-in-law before they are all washed away."

Two months after the B.X. completed her maiden voyage, the *Chilcotin* was ready. She arrived at Quesnel on August 17, her supporters still boasting that she was faster than the B.X. On the latter point the *Cariboo Observer* commented: ". . . this remains to be demonstrated, and will excite considerable interest among the enthusiastic adherents of both lines."

The *Chilcotin* reached South Fort George without incident but on her return was badly damaged in Fort George Canyon and beached for the rest of the season. On October 1 the B.X. was also battered out of service when she struck a rock above the Canyon. A 60-foot long, 3-foot wide section was gashed from her hull but watertight compartments kept her afloat until Captain Browne beached her. Three weeks later she was back in service. During the same period both *Charlotte* and *Chilco* were wrecked.

The *Charlotte*'s accident was unusual. While steaming down Fort George Canyon she started settling in the water. There had been no shudder to indicate that she had banged a reef; nevertheless, she was obviously sinking. Captain D. A. Foster quickly beached her, remaining in the pilothouse until she keeled over so far he had to escape through a window. The engineer, meanwhile, stayed at the throttle until water reached his neck. As one newspaper commented: "They were able through their coolness and bravery to prevent a panic." The vessel was salvaged but her hull was waterlogged and she was abandoned at Quesnel.

The *Chilco*, actually *Nechacco* with a new name, met disaster on her last trip of the season. A few miles above Cottonwood Canyon a steampipe blew and she drifted onto a rock. She was beached but repairs couldn't be completed until spring. Next April after river ice cleared she sailed for Quesnel and a major overhaul. As she nosed into Cottonwood Canyon, Captain George Ritchie was dismayed to see the lower end blocked with ice. He swung upstream but another pipe blew and the powerless vessel drifted into the canyon. Realizing that the situation was hopeless, Ritchie shouted orders to abandon ship. The crew were barely clear when she ground into the ice, capsized, and disappeared without trace.

Loss of the two vessels left only four for the 1911 season: B.X., *Quesnel*, *Fort Fraser*, and *Chilcotin*. The latter vessel proved to be greatly over-rated. She had to be lined through the Canyons and at high water couldn't complete a trip a week to South Fort George. The B.X., on the other hand, easily maintained a twice-weekly service up the river. This schedule was apparently profitable since on July 29 the *Fort George Herald* reported that ". . . the steamer B.X. . . . is said to have cleaned up about $15,000 during the first month's run this season."

The 1912 season promised to be equally profitable. From the east rails for the Grand Trunk Pacific reached B.C., and at the head of navigation only 53 miles from the Alberta border mushroomed a shantytown called Tete Jaune Cache. To move the massive tonnage of freight appeared three new sternweelers. They were *B.C. Express*, built by the B.C. Express Company to ply from South Fort George to Tete Jaune Cache, and *Operator* and *Conveyor*.

The latter two had originally been used on Skeena River by the railway contractors. With completion of the Skeena portion of the line they were dismantled at Victoria and their machinery hauled by rail via Jasper to Red Pass just inside the B.C. border. In all there were 10 car loads, including two 50,000-pound boilers. From Red Pass the tons of parts were dragged by mules over a 25-mile, roller-coaster tote road to a shipyard hacked from the bank of the Fraser River one mile east of Tete Jaune Cache. Moving the boilers alone took a week and the life of a construction worker.

The vessels, launched May 12, 1912, were the largest to appear on the Upper Fraser. Each could carry 200 passen-

gers, 200 tons of freight, and push a barge with another 100 tons. They were a snug fit for the river; in fact, at one point the bank was shovelled out so that they could squeeze around a bend.

When navigation season opened, the *Fort George Herald* reported that value of steamers on the Upper Fraser was some $350,000. On the whole, however, 1912 was not successful. The river dropped to an extremely low level, exposing a host of new bars and reefs. The *Chilcotin* punctured herself three times on one trip between Soda Creek and Fort George, and even the *B.X.* had problems, twice ramming the same rock in Fort George Canyon. The *Fort George Herald* commented: "The B.X. which last year ran uninterruptedly all season without even taking the paint off her sides, this year is meeting with every possible impediment in the river and every sunken rock appears to challenge her progress." Because of low water the *B.C. Express* was marooned for over a month, and the *Operator* and *Conveyor* withdrawn from service early in September.

By contrast, next season surged with action. Rail construction between Fort George and Tete Jaune Cache alone employed 5,000 men, settlers moved up the Cariboo Road by hundreds, and the communities of South Fort George and Fort George had grown to 1,500 each. Fort George was a fairly quiet residential town but South Fort George operated in the tradition of the wild west. Its red light district flourished and in Albert Johnson's Northern Hotel men stood five and six deep in front of a bar 90 feet long. Bartenders worked twelve a shift, and though whisky was only .25 cents a drink, liquor sales reached $7,000 a day. On at least one upstream trip liquor comprised the entire cargo of the *B.X.*— 100 tons of rum, whisky, champagne and similar spirits.

In 1913 appeared the last sternwheeler built on the Upper Fraser. She was *Robert C. Hammond,* a small vessel whose purpose was to support Hammond's lavish claim that sternwheelers called regularly at his community. Actually, sand bars prevented vessels reaching Fort George except at high-water, and a $50 bonus offered to B.C. Express Company

At upper left Captain Bonser, in the stripe shirt, with a party of settlers he has just landed on the bank of the Nechako River in 1910. At left the Fort Fraser lines herself up White Mud Rapids on the Nechako River.

Above is a scow in the Grand Canyon of the Upper Fraser River in 1913. Manned by six to eight men, the scows drifted 315 miles from Tete Jaune Cache to Fort George in about five days if the crew was lucky. Each scow cost about $300 to build and carried some 25 tons of freight at $70 a ton. Life for the 1,500 "River Hogs" who crewed them was as perilous as that many later experienced in the trenches of France. Number drowned is unknown, but at least 50 died in the Grand Canyon alone during 1913.

whenever the *B.X.* steamed to the townsite was collected infrequently. The editor of the *Fort George Herald* wasn't impressed with the new vessel, commenting: "Doubtless there will be times when the *Robert C. Hammond* will have some difficulty, owing to thin water, in reaching her home port, but 'We should worry.' At such times the Fort George band, with a few variations, can play a stanza or two of that delightful ballad 'Waiting for the *Robert E. Lee*'."

Even if the *Hammond* could reach home port only at intervals, she and the other vessels prospered during 1913. The *B.C. Express* for instance, running a weekly service on the 315-mile section between South Fort George and Tete Jaune Cache, netted $5,000 a week.

She maintained this schedule largely because of her skillful captain, J. E. Bucey. Among obstacles were seven-mile-long Giscome Rapids, Goat River Rapids, and the Grand Canyon, a fearsome, double slash through volcanic rock just over 100 miles upstream from Fort George. Here the river constricts to a quarter of normal, the compressed water squirting through the cleft rock with such velocity that sternwheelers, engines full astern, careened through at 15 miles an hour. Below this gut was another stretch described by one traveller as a "cavernous opening scarcely fifty feet wide, presenting a specter of somber, awful grandeur. It was like peering into a huge vault. . . ." At the mouth the entire river became a whirlpool, its vortex easily swallowing complete trees in a pulsing confusion of foam. During 1913, its swirling waters

The Quesnel *bringing the first white women to Fort George on May 1, 1910. One of her captains was Donald Arthur 'Cap' Foster who arrived in Cariboo in 1898. During the sternwheel era he was master of many vessels, including the Chilcotin, Charlotte, and Quesnel. He was also the last active sternwheel skipper on the Upper Fraser. Apart from overseas service with the Royal Engineers during World War I, he lived in the Cariboo all his life and is buried in Quesnel. The* Quesnel *was the last sternwheeler to sail the Upper Fraser River.*

drowned dozens of men, the crews of scows used for freighting supplies downstream.

The scows, which averaged 40 feet long by 16 feet with a capacity of 25 tons, were launched at Tete Jaune Cache and let drift downstream, their crew trying to control them with a pole at the stern. One day alone $250,000 in merchandise was set adrift, with the railway construction firm sending 100 scows a day downstream. In the first few weeks of the season, over 20 men were drowned in Grand Canyon alone and by July goods lost exceeded $100,000.

Despite hazards of riding the tumultous waters of the Grand Canyon, Captain Bucey skimmed through regularly, although at times only his superb skill prevented disaster. Once when the *B.C. Express* was challenging the whirlpool a 70-foot-long tree jammed her rudders and she swung out of control. Since towering rock walls prevented a deckhand getting ashore and snubbing her to a tree, Bucey had only the sternwheel for control. By varying its revolutions he was able to shepherd his vessel safely downstream. The only

apparent casualty was a man who leaped onto a ledge when a whirlpool slammed the boat into the rock wall. Although no one expected to see him again, Bucey sent four crewmen back to check. The man was still there, the giant whirlpool gurgling six feet below him, rock cliff towering 70 feet above. Aided by 200 feet of line, the crew rescued him, although one had to be lowered down the cliff to tie the rope around the petrified passenger.

Hazards of nature, however, were only part of Captain Bucey's problems. On one trip 20 tough construction workers refused to pay their fare. The captain promptly nosed his vessel ashore, went to the group and ordered the ringleader tossed overboard, even though they outnumbered his crew. Before the startled troublemaker could object, he was battling the icy current. Without a glance at him Bucey returned to his wheelhouse and continued downstream, letting the man reach shore as best he could. Thereafter, the purser had no difficulty collecting fares.

On a trip later in the summer Captain Bucey encountered

an obstacle that proved permanent. At Mile 141 above Fort George a bridge construction crew without warning strung a low cable across the river, blocking navigation. Bucey threatened to blast his way through with a shotgun but was persuaded not to and returned to South Fort George.

In the railway company's original plans, they agreed to build bridges that would not impede navigation. It was now obvious that the agreement would be ignored. Although the B.C. Express Company started legal action, construction of the bridge and another downstream continued, ending navigation on 200 miles of river.

The Express Company, however, wasn't the only victim of the multi-million dollar Grand Trunk Pacific railway. The autumn of 1913 climaxed development of both South Fort George and Fort George. The Railway Development Company purchased an Indian reservation between South Fort George and Fort George and started a third townsite, Prince George. Thereafter the original settlements waned and died.

Arrival of the first train to Prince George on January 27, 1914, changed a transportation pattern set in 1858 when Yale and Port Douglas on the Lower Fraser became portals to Cariboo and Central B.C. In 1886 they in turn were bypassed when completion of the C.P.R. made Ashcroft entry point; now Prince George would become the hub.

The first train was also mortal for Upper Fraser sternwheelers, although their usefulness had not yet ended. Construction started on a new railway, the Pacific Great Eastern, to link Prince George and Vancouver. By October, 1914 nearly 5,000 men were working on the right-of-way, with sternwheelers again carrying capacity loads.

Two of them were B.X. and Conveyor, both considered the fastest on the river. But not until a day in July, 1914 when they arrived at Soda Creek and prepared to leave for Prince George next morning did they have a chance to race. Captain Shannon of the Conveyor promptly suggested that they race for an hour and the lead vessel be declared speed queen. Captain Browne of the B.X. accepted, although he had just loaded 40 tons of cargo and mail, and would have to make his regular calls. Conveyor, on the other hand, was empty with no calls.

The race started at dawn, and a complete description was written for the B.C. Historical Quarterly by Willis J. West, superintendent of the B.C. Express Company. Here is a condensed version:

". . . the B.X. steamed around a bend and there, brilliantly lighted, was the Conveyor. As the B.X. drew near, Browne, hearing the safety-valve of the Conveyor blowing, realized that her boiler had a full head of steam and that she was ready for the start of the contest. When the B.X. was still

South Fort George at its peak development in 1914, and freight wagons on the Cariboo Road. Everything from eggs to champagne came by wagon, with probably the heaviest item freighted up the road the Charlotte's boiler. It was 20 feet long, 18 in circumference, and weighed over seven tons. A veteran teamster, Luly Hautier, tackled the hauling job. With pioneer nonchalance he hooked 16 mules to an iron-axled bull wagon and creaked slowly up the torturous hill leading from Ashcroft. Despite obstacles which included wheels buckling under the strain, he trundled slowly northward and six weeks and 210 miles later rumbled down the hill to the sternwheeler ways at Quesnel.

The upper photo shows the Operator, a construction locomotive on her foredeck, at Mile 49 on the Upper Fraser. Above, waiting for the B.X. at Quesnel, June 1913. The B.X. made two trips a week to South Fort George. She left Soda Creek at 3 a.m., reached Quesnel about noon, then steamed until dark. Since night navigation was too risky, she tied up until morning, and arrived at South Fort George about 11 o'clock. On the return she left at 7 a.m. and arrived at Soda Creek about 4:30 in the afternoon. Fare was $17.50, meals 75¢ each. A lower berth was $1.50; an upper, $1.00.

CHAPTER FIVE

Skeena and Stikine Rivers

The Indians called her 'K-shian, water of the clouds.' The riverboatmen, less poetic, called her an unpredictable wench. By temperament she is nervous and unstable, impatient to leave her birthplace in the storm-shrouded rock spires of the Skeena Mountains, hurrying to tidewater with a determination that made her the West's fastest flowing major waterway. Some sternwheel skippers credited her with being among the toughest of North America's navigable rivers. Others disagreed, saying she wasn't among the toughest; she was the toughest. She could rise 17 feet in a day, fluctuate 60 feet between high and low water, puncture a sternwheeler's planking in a dozen rapid-torn canyons or rock-strewn rapids. "We don't navigate the river," one veteran skipper observed, "we juggle our way down."

Pioneer sternwheeler on the Skeena was the *Union*, a 60-foot-long vessel which left Victoria on June 11, 1864 with four passengers and 20 tons of freight. Her owner, Captain Tom Coffin, felt that his light craft could trade into waters unapproachable to larger ones. The venture, however, was unsuccessful, although next year he was back, his vessel chartered by Collins Overland Telegraph, a firm building an around-the-world telegraph line via B.C., Yukon, Alaska and Siberia. This time the *Union* battled upstream 90 miles, but could go no further.

During the winter, the Telegraph Company built a sternwheeler especially for northern rivers. She was the *Mumford*, and under Captain Coffin, left Victoria for the Skeena on July 5, 1866. She returned in August, with the *Victoria Colonist* reporting: "She ascended the Skeena River two or three times, having gone up a distance of 110 miles, but found navigation very torturous and difficult."

Charles Morrison, one of those aboard, wrote an account of the trip which indicates just how torturous navigation was. At one canyon, he noted: "Captain Coffin wedged the safety valve down, we had all line out and heaving on the

The Hazelton on the Skeena in 1907. During frontier days, sternwheelers were often the only source of refreshment for those challenging the wilderness. On the Skeena for some 180 miles between Port Essington and Hazelton the pioneer Caledonia had the only bar and whenever she stopped, trappers, prospectors, and others materialized from the woods to patronize her.

windlass, I was busy with a bucksaw sawing short lengths of wood to fill the furnace; they threw a five gallon tin of lard into the furnace, all the cook's slush and several sides of fat bacon, the steam gauge had gone to 'No man's land', the line parted and we gave up, dropped down a few yards and tied up, the Chief Engineer knocked away the lever, opened the valve, threw the fire overboard and we were at peace."

Morrison also commented on passenger facilities, not exactly first cabin. "We had to anchor several times to go ashore to cut wood as the steamer, heavily loaded, had very little room for fuel. The weather was fine and the scenery grand; the food was good, but the boat only had sleeping accommodation for the ship's company; we, the passengers, had to pick a soft plank every night to lay our blankets on, which also was not grand . . ."

The *Mumford* arrived back in New Westminster in October, and despite her difficulties had delivered to Skeena River 150 miles of material for the line and 12,000 rations

for workmen. Unfortunately for backers of the Collins project, that year a cable was successfully laid under the Atlantic Ocean, outmoding the around-the-world telegraph. The entire line north of Quesnel was abandoned and sternwheel service on the Skeena temporarily ended.

Next flurry was in 1870-71 when gold was discovered in Omineca country. One means of access was to ascend the Skeena 180 miles to a trading post called Hazelton. From there a trail led 50 miles to Fort Babine on Babine Lake, 30 miles to Takla Lake, then another 35 miles to the Omineca diggings. Among the hundreds of gold seekers was, as might be expected, Captain William Moore.

But in contrast to his Fraser and Stikine days the captain wasn't commanding a sternwheeler. He was still nearly broke, so with his sons operated a pack train of 26 horses over the Babine Trail. Then in the winter of 1872 he contracted with the H.B.C. to supply their post at Hazelton. At Port Essington, a new settlement forming near the mouth of the Skeena, Moore and his three sons built two barges.

The Inlander *bound for Hazelton lines up Kitselas Canyon. After a winter of isolation, arrival of the first boat in spring was excuse for a celebration to upriver communities. "When we landed at Hazelton, the whole town— whites, Indians and dogs—were down to meet us," re-* called Wiggs O'Neill. "When the ship blew her whistle, everyone waved and cheered and the dogs sat on their hind ends and howled. The arrival of the boat meant fresh provisions, including fruit and case eggs, and a fresh supply of liquor for the Hudson's Bay stone cellar."

With a crew of 12 Indians in each, plus two canoes with another six Indians, they started rowing, poling, and towing upstream. Besides the grueling work, there were other hazards. Kitseguecla Rapids, where 12 miners drowned the previous autumn, were a formidable barrier, and adding to natural dangers were hostile Indians. They attacked a party of some 25 miners, killing one and wounding two, and threatened Moore and his party. The captain, however, never shirked a challenge. He armed his group and pushed onward, eventually reaching Hazelton in safety. On the return trip the Indians attacked, one bullet wounding a crewman in the leg, another smacking the steering oar six inches from Moore's hand.

The Omineca excitement, however, was fleeting and traffic soon dwindled. Moore and his sons left for a new area, the Cassiar, where they would find their golden rainbow.

Another man prominent in the supply route to Omineca was Robert Cunningham, a strong-willed Irishman. Origin-ally he came to the north coast to serve the Church Mission-ary Society at the Indian settlement of Metlakatla. After two years he left and joined the H.B.C. at Fort Simpson, a coastal trading post 40 miles north of the Skeena. Then in 1870 he left the H.B.C. to trade independently and eventually start a community which he named Port Essington. It was strategically located on the south bank of the Skeena, close enough to tidewater so that coastal vessels could call, yet far enough inland to serve the river. Even the H.B.C. acknowledged their former employee's astuteness. They bought property and started supplying posts as far inland as Stuart Lake via the Skeena instead of the Fraser River.

In due course, though, Company managers realized that freighting supplies 180 miles from Port Essington to Hazelton by canoe was expensive, uncertain, and slow. On October 17, 1888, Junior Chief Trader R. H. Hall wrote ". . . without a Steamer the Skeena Route cannot be largely utilized for New Caledonia."

As a result of his report, in September, 1889, the Company

The smallest sternwheeler to appear on the Skeena was the Craigflower, upper left. She could sail in six inches of water, but was underpowered and turned back a few miles above Kitwanga. Her owner brought her north because of a hot tip on money to be made, but all she earned was a nickname—Cauliflower.

The photo at left shows the Pheasant on the Skeena River in 1906. Later in the year on her last trip of the season she broke her back in Red Rock Canyon. It was the first loss for her pioneer captain, J. H. Bonser. Mrs. E. M. Whit-low, who went to Kitselas Canyon in 1903 and lived there for over 60 years, recalls that Captain Bonser "was a friendly man and very popular among the old pioneers." The Omineca, above, at full steam as she approaches swift water. A correspondent bound upstream wrote of a canyon that they "approached with steam roaring through the safety valve, the funnel belching flames, and smoke in clouds and the whole vessel vibrating to the shaking of the engines . . . ."

hired Captain George Odin, veteran Fraser River stern-wheeler skipper, to survey the Skeena. His report was favorable and on November 29, 1890, the *Victoria Colonist* noted that the H.B.C. "will make the experiment of navigating the Skeena River in the spring." The paper also added, by way of respect for Skeena's reputation: "As Yet, the venture can only be regarded in the light of an experiment, as the dangers of navigating the Skeena are such that the loss of the new boat on her first trip would not be a surprise."

On February 28, 1891, the new vessel, christened *Caledonia*, was launched at New Westminster and taken to Victoria for installation of machinery. On April 4 the *Victoria Colonist* announced that "She is a Clipper." Then after her trials a few days later, reported: "The steamer proved steady, and her engines ran smoothly. . . . Although strength, not speed, is a primary object sought, a speed of 16 miles an hour was attained."

Under Captain George Odin she made her first successful

trip to Hazelton in May, taking nine days to beat her way upstream. But since such a trip was considered impossible, the H.B.C. was satisfied. Captain Odin's son, Frank, assumed command and the vessel served not only on the Skeena but also the Nass and north-coastal B.C.

One of her skippers was J. H. Bonser, a man with considerable whitewater experience from the Lewis River. He reported that while she had ample power, a somewhat stubby design made her hard to handle. Consequently, in 1895 when she went into winter quarters at Port Simpson she was sawn in half and 30 feet spliced into her. Thereafter she was much more manoeuverable.

It was Captain Bonser, too, who christened the 11 major rapids and canyons that laced the 180 miles of Skeena from tidewater to Hazelton. In general he chose names which matched the temperament of the obstacle. At the Whirly Gig cross currents shook a sternwheeler like gravel in a prospector's gold pan; at the Hornet's Nest the vessels ran a gauntlet of boulders; Sheep Rapids was a section where white water resembled galloping sheep; while at the Devil's Elbow the river flowed straight into a rock bluff then veered abruptly right—a section unnerving to even the most seasoned traveller.

To aid sternwheelers fight up the most turbulent rapids, ringbolts were anchored in the canyon walls. With their cable and steam capstan, the vessels hauled themselves up in a hand-over-hand manner, a procedure known as *lining*. In sections where there were rapids but no rock to anchor a ringbolt, a *deadman* was used. This device was simply a log dug into the gravel at the head of the rapids and anchored. From the deadman downstream ran a cable buoyed with a block of wood. Upstream bound vessels simply picked up the cable and lined themselves up the rapids. At the crest the buoyed cable was dropped overboard where it floated downstream ready for the next vessel.

On one trip up the Skeena a passenger was C. H. French, who later became H.B.C. district manager for B.C. In an article in *The Beaver* he recounted: "The excitement—the thrill—that one gets when passing through the canyons of the Skeena is beyond word-picturing.

"Entering the Little Canyon from the lower end, one gets the impression that he is starting through a subterranean passage, because of the towering, straight walls—so high that darkness appears to be gathering.

"After proceeding a little further one notes that the "boils" (whirlpools) are getting larger and if you look over the side of the ship you will note that an extra large "boil" has struck the steamer right on the stem, and has caused her to settle until the water is rushing in over the bow. Suddenly the "boil" has careened the boat to one side and has shifted to her quarter. The crew, with large rope bumper, rush to the side opposite the boil so that in case the captain is not able to straighten the boat up they will be able to swing the bumpers between the guard of the steamer and the rough, jagged walls of the canyon.

On B.C.'s rivers, passengers saw wildlife that included moose, bear, and deer. Along the Skeena, mountain goat were prevalent, with a traveller on the Port Simpson, opposite, reporting that "we presently saw three of them walking and running high up on the mountainside."

"Now the "boil" has reached amidships just under where you are standing, and when you look down into it (they could be 20 and more feet deep) and feel the boat settling under you, you wonder if there is really any bottom to it and whether the boat will be sucked under or whether she will eventually rise.

"Probably when the guard of the boat is under water and the decks are actually flooded, the boil will shift a trifle to one side. Then the boat will immediately float up and go along."

On the trip the paddlewheel was damaged and the boat stopped for repairs. A large Indian canoe came downstream and, wrote Mr. French: "We endeavored both by signs and shouting to warn the crew that they should not enter the canyon, but the only reply they gave us was to paddle harder and in a flash this large war canoe with a crew of sixteen Indians shot into the canyon and out of our sight.

"Neither the canoe nor any of its crew were ever found, and it can only be surmised that one of those large "boils" took the craft and held it, gradually sucking it lower until at a certain point the canoe would stand straight on end and disappear, the crew either being held in the eddy or carried down and deposited underneath the large drift piles."

Despite hazards of the Skeena, the *Caledonia* served northern coastal waters for seven seasons, then on December 28, 1897, the *Victoria Colonist* noted that she "will return to Victoria to be torn to pieces. Her machinery is wanted for a new boat."

Hastening the Company's decision was the Klondike stampede. One route to Yukon was via Skeena River, another via the Stikine. The latter route gained prominence when the Canadian Government stated that a railroad would link Stikine River to Yukon. This announcement resulted in various companies building or planning to build a fleet of some 40 sternwheelers to handle expected Stikine traffic. The railway, unfortunately, became a political football and died. So did the sternwheeler fleet, although by then over a dozen were ready.

On the Skeena, however, the H.B.C.'s new vessel, again called *Caledonia,* was kept busy. The surge to Klondike had awakened the north. It also made Robert Cunningham, whose business interests now included everything from salmon canning to lumbering, decide to add a sternwheeler to his enterprises. He promptly hired Captain Bonser from the H.B.C. and bought the *Monte Cristo,* originally built for the Stikine River.

Residents along the Skeena waited for rivalry to develop but the H.B.C. ignored their former employee. They had another new vessel, *Strathcona,* which they felt could more than compete. Besides that, there was freight enough for both firms. Spurred by the Klondike rush, the Canadian Government was building a telegraph line from Quesnel to Dawson City, with Hazelton a main supply base.

But that winter Cunningham jolted the lofty H.B.C. He sent Captain Bonser to Victoria to design a sternwheeler

Top photo shows Port Essington in 1908. By then it had a population of several hundred, with hotels, saloons, town hall, bakery, canneries and other businesses. Pioneer community was Port Simpson, center, but it and Port Essington were superseded by Prince Rupert, opposite, about 1909.

especially for the Skeena. On Friday, April 26, 1901, the *Victoria Colonist* reported that the new vessel, *Hazelton,* "... is a great success...." The paper added that the coming season on the Skeena was expected to be one of great activity, with every town and village busy. "Port Essington is first and foremost among the coming centres of civilization on the northern coast of B.C. Many new buildings are under construction and the two new hotels just completed are a great addition to the town...."

The *Hazelton* quickly proved superior to the H.B.C. vessels. In her first season she made 13 trips to Hazelton, steaming upstream in about 40 hours, returning in 10. Since the H.B.C. vessels couldn't compete, the firm ordered a new sternwheeler. She was the *Mount Royal,* a vessel destined to bring intense rivalry—and tragedy—to the Skeena.

She was built at Victoria and scheduled for launching at 3:45, April 9, 1902. But instead of sliding smoothly down the ways, she hung up. Workmen freed her in two hours and again she started to the bay; only this time she lurched

into the bank. Not for several days could she be coaxed into the water. To sailors, the launch was an ill-omen.

By June she completed trials and headed to Skeena. Immediately, competition flared. In July, Cunningham's *Hazelton* made the round trip from Port Essington to Hazelton in 2 days, 7 hours, and 55 minutes. Two days later *Mount Royal* clipped 1 hour and 40 minutes from this time. Then the *Hazelton* scooted up and back in 47 hours. "Beat the other boat" became a standing order. Skippers required no encouraging, sailing at times with cargo left on the dock in order to beat the other. The rivalry increased like summer heat, then peaked with the suddenness of a lightning bolt.

"STEAMBOAT FIGHT ON THE SKEENA" headlined the *Vancouver Province* on May 24, 1904, followed by news that "... the green foliage on the trees along the bank of the river was shrivelled by the sulphurous language that was hurled from one boat to the other." More than language was hurled. One skipper left his pilothouse for a rifle to shoot his rival.

Hazelton, sternwheel terminus on the Upper Skeena. The community, though small, was vital to a far-flung area. On July 18, 1904, a correspondent for the Skeena District News reported that the "people of the surrounding country for hundreds of miles get their supplies at Hazelton." At upper *right Inlander leaves Prince Rupert for the Skeena. Even though she arrived when sternwheel days were waning and operated only one full season out of three, she paid shareholders 50 per cent dividends the first year, 150 per cent the second, and 50 per cent the third.*

The Hazelton and Omineca at Hazelton. Sternwheelers and their crews were considered one of the family to pioneer residents. On October 15, 1910, the Omineca Herald reported: "Captain Gardiner and officers of the steamer Hazelton entertained the townspeople Friday evening at the Omineca Hotel, giving a dance and supper that was out of the ordinary in this part of the country. . . . An elaborate supper was served . . . and following that dancing resumed until nearly 3 o'clock in the morning. Everyone attending pronounced the affair a great success. . . ."

Trigger for the uproar was the desire of both skippers to be first of the season to Hazelton. The *Hazelton* completed loading first but unknown to Captain Bonser, *Mount Royal* was nearly ready. At Hardscrabble Rapids, about 105 miles upstream, Captain Bonser pulled ashore for fuel. While the four-foot chunks of wood were being stowed aboard, a column of smoke appeared downstream. As Walter Warner, chief steward on the *Hazelton* later recalled, "We had no idea the *Mount Royal* had started . . . and as the telegraph operators had been warned not to say a word . . . it was quite a surprise. We had about half the wood on board when Captain Bonser gave a toot to let go lines. . . ."

Coming up in fairly slack water, the *Mount Royal* quickly gained and soon the vessels were bow to bow—smoke, steam, and cinders belching skywards; paddlewheels frothing rapids white, passengers urging their vessels forward. Gradually *Mount Royal* thrust ahead, then suddenly was jolted as *Hazelton's* bow crunched into her starboard quarter. Fortunately her overhanging main deck absorbed the blow or the *Hazelton* could have slashed into her engine room, with deadly results.

As it was, the current started carrying both vessels towards the rocks, *Hazelton* again butting her rival like a frisky billy goat. Finally, the *Mount Royal* was broadside to the current, then swung free. She lost steerage way and the current carried her downstream, bow first. Meanwhile the *Hazelton* surged upstream, tooting her whistle and wagging her stern as she threshed triumphantly over the rapids.

The ramming incident was discussed along the river for weeks, some blaming one skipper, some the other. But by the time the leaves flared yellow the event was history, except to Captain Johnson, who was probably still nettled at the memory of the *Hazelton* defiantly wagging her stern as she crested the rapids. When the season closed he charged that Captain Bonser "deliberately and with malice run his vessel into the *Mount Royal* with the purpose of injuring the latter craft." He claimed, among other things, that Bonser "boasted of his achievement after the act." In defence, Captain Bonser said that the collision was an accident.

As a result of the charges, the Federal Department of Marine investigated, with Captain Gaudin in charge. As the investigation proceeded, those involved soon realized that neither captain was exactly innocent. During the incident Captain Johnson had left the helm to find a rifle to shoot his rival, thus exposing his passengers and crew to grave risk. In the end Captain Gaudin ruled that both captains were to blame, with Johnson in particular committing a great dereliction of duty by leaving the helm of his vessel unattended. The captains were reprimanded and the case closed.

One thing that the incident did emphasize to both the Bay and Cunningham was that rivalry was profitless. Consequently, they "had a meeting" and reached an understanding. According to old-timers, the Bay agreed to pay Cunningham $2,500 to tie up his vessel, to haul his freight free, and to purchase the *Hazelton* if traffic warranted. This option they later exercised.

As a result of the consolidation, Captain Bonser was without a vessel. In 1906 he took command of the *Pheasant*, a small sternwheeler so underpowered that local wags nicknamed her the *Chicken* because she had to scratch so hard to get up the rapids. Her career on the Skeena was brief. That

autumn on her last trip of the season she was wrecked in Redrock Canyon. It was Captain Bonser's first loss. Next year his former rival, Captain Johnson, also lost his first vessel—with tragic results.

He was still in command of *Mount Royal*, and on the afternoon of July 6 reached Kitselas Canyon, a mile-long, rock-studded chute 93 miles downstream from Hazelton. Here the river splits into three channels, the rock outcrops acting as a dam. A one-foot rise in river level can raise water level five feet at the head of the canyon, while fluctuation between high and low water in the canyon reaches 60 feet. Only two of the three channels were navigable, and down them the vessels shot at full speed to maintain steerageway.

As the *Mount Royal* approached the center channel on her tragic trip, a gust of wind spun her into a rock pillar called Ringbolt Island. The 10 knot current swung her stern to the opposite bank, jamming her crossways in the channel. Fortunately she held fast while passengers and crew got ashore.

The Caledonia, *upper right, and the* Strathcona, *above, were the second and third sternwheelers which the Hudson's Bay Company built for service on the Skeena and Upper Coast. In the summer of 1908 the* Caledonia *demonstrated the fearful punishment that a sternwheeler could absorb and survive. She gashed a 30-foot-long hole in her hull on a rock downstream from Port Essington in an area of the river known as the Skeena Boneyard. She was pulled off this obstacle but in backing up struck another submerged rock. Water poured in, extinguished her fire, and she sank, leaving only her upperworks and pilothouse above the water. She was raised and beached at Port Essington and three weeks later was back in service.*

At times, however, vessels were battered so badly that repairs were impossible. Such was the fate of the Northwest, *opposite. In 1907 while bound for Hazelton she struck a rock and was totally wrecked. Fortunately, big boulders in the channel aided passengers and crew to scramble safely to the bank of the Skeena River.*

The vessel, meanwhile, creaked and bucked as the water buffeted her, but seemed to be withstanding the pressure, leading Captain Johnson to believe that she could be saved. With 10 crewmen he returned aboard. In his book *Steamboat Days On the Skeena River,* Wiggs O'Neill, who was associated with Skeena sternwheelers for many years, wrote: "The captain decided that by running a cable through a snatch block at the stern and up to the capstan on the bow he could pull the stern back up and over against Ringbolt Island. They just got nicely started and it looked promising when her king post jumped off its footing in the hold and went through her bottom.

"She buckled in the middle, the strong current came over her guard and she rolled over bottom up and broke in the middle. . . ." Of those who returned aboard, six drowned, including the first officer.

Residents of the small community of Kitselas at the Canyon's mouth learned of the tragedy when hundreds of pieces of wreckage floated downstream. One large chunk of hull grounded on a bar. George Little, who later founded the community of Terrace, and a companion paddled over to the hull. They clambered aboard and were astonished to see a hand wave from a hole in the planking. It was the chief engineer, Ben Maddigan. He had been washed into the bilge when the vessel capsized, and although drenched in grime and oil, was unhurt.

"There must have been some air down there," George Little commented, after they had chopped him free.

"I don't know about air," said the engineer, squeezing grease and cylinder oil from his once white beard, "but there was one hell of a lot of water!"

Two months later the river claimed another sternwheeler, the *Northwest* ". . . with a jar and crash that sounded like workmen prying boards from the sides of a building we . . . struck a rock," wrote a passenger. Everyone on board got ashore safely where they watched the river "grapple with the battered hulk until with one mighty sweep the ship went over on its side . . . as the waters surged about the ship,

extinguishing the fires beneath the boilers, it seemed as if a shriek from some huge monster was being echoed and re-echoed along the banks of the stream."

Since much of the *Northwest's* cargo was the winter liquor supply for upriver points, her loss was personal and serious to many residents. On top of this, the *Hazelton*, the only remaining vessel, struck a bar and was stranded. Fortunately, after losing the *Mount Royal*, the H.B.C. started refitting the *Caledonia* and before freeze-up she freighted upstream bottled goods sufficient to brighten the long winter evenings.

Mr. J. C. Loutet, who was at one time manager of the H.B.C. store at Hazelton, remembers the annual arrival of the season's bottled goods. There would be cases of champagne and many varieties of wine; wooden barrels full of beer in quart bottles; and 42 gallon kegs of rum, scotch, rye, and gin. "Rum was $1 a bottle if drawn from the cask," he recalls. "When you entered a bar and called for a drink, a highly polished glass was put by you and a bottle of what-

ever you were drinking. You poured your own and the privilege was never abused."

Other supplies included flour in 49 and 98 pound bags; sugar in 20's, 50's and 100's; matts of rice; dried apricots, peaches, apples and prunes in wooden boxes weighing about 22 pounds; and wooden tubs of candy. Then there would be gallon tins of fruit, four-pound tins of jams, slabs of bacon, whole hams, and dried beans, peas and similar produce.

The Port Simpson in Kitselas Canyon, a section of the Skeena so formidable that sternwheelers frequently let themselves down by cable. On July 31, 1907, a Victoria Colonist correspondent wrote ". . . Indians who constitute the crews of the river vessels . . . leap from rocks or scramble along narrow ledges overhanging the seething water with the sure-footed agility of mountain goats. They make wild dashes . . . through the boiling torrent in small boats, carrying with them the cable; they plunge waist deep . . . where a misstep could place them at the mercy of the cruel waters. . . ."

Shortly after the *Caledonia* made her last trip in 1907 the H.B.C. sold her and ordered a replacement to take advantage of a new development. Construction was underway on a transcontinental railway—the Grand Trunk Pacific—from Winnipeg across Central B.C. to tidewater. Western terminus was a small island just north of the Skeena estuary where a port called Prince Rupert was hacked from forest, rock, and muskeg. President of the line was Charles Melville

Hays, a "super-salesman, visionary, and man of action." His visionary plans included building Prince Rupert into a major seaport terminus of both coastal and trans-Pacific shipping lines. The city would have a $3,000,000 shipyard, drydock capable of servicing 20,000 ton vessels, and a population of 50,000. Unfortunately, an iceberg in the North Atlantic was to decree otherwise.

For now, however, all was bustle. On January 30, 1908, the *Victoria Colonist* reported that there "will be five, possibly six steamers in service on the Skeena River this summer." One of them was the new H.B.C. vessel, *Port Simpson*, while two others, *Distributor* and *Skeena,* were built for the railway construction firm of Foley Bros., Welch and Stewart.

This firm also bought the veteran *Omineca* but that summer she was wrecked below Port Essington. She was beached and her machinery installed in a new vessel also called *Omineca*. She appeared next year with two sister ships, *Operator* and *Conveyor*, giving the construction firm a fleet of five sternwheelers.

The Mount Royal, *launched at Victoria in April 1902, was the finest sternwheeler to appear on the Skeena. Built of Douglas fir and eastern oak at a cost of $30,000, she had stateroom accommodation for 100 passengers and cabin room for 200. Empty she could sail in only 18 inches of water; fully laden with cargo and passengers needed only 18 more. She had the reputation of being the fastest and most powerful riverboat ever built in Victoria and always maintained her supremacy as the fastest steamer on the Skeena. She was wrecked in Kitselas Canyon, opposite.*

The Ogilvie, at top, was one of a fleet planned by the C.P.R. to ply the Stikine River as part of the "All-Canadian" route to Klondike in 1898.

The workhorses of the Grand Trunk Pacific Railway construction fleet—the Skeena, Conveyor, Distributor and Omineca— leave Prince Rupert for the Skeena River.

The construction company vessels were workhorses that hauled tens of thousands of tons of railway construction material. The 186-mile section from Hazelton to Prince Rupert was the most difficult of the entire route across the West. One section of 60 miles was almost solid rock, and to get past Kitselas Canyon where *Mount Royal* was wrecked, tunnels 400, 700, and 1,100 feet long were necessary. The route was so difficult that to locate 186 miles of track, over 12,000 miles of surveys and trial lines were run, while construction of the 80-mile section from Prince Rupert to Kitselas Canyon alone required 12 million pounds of

---

When rail construction ended, the Skeena sailed south to the Lower Fraser River area. By then throughout the province pioneers had established farms and ranches, built schools and founded communities that today are cities. Women and children were now part of the frontier, a change from conditions short years before when women passengers on sternwheelers were so infrequent that they "were regarded with much wondering curiosity, and some amount of chivalric respect by the miners, who, with the greatest self-denial, actually refrained from swearing within earshot, or squirting tobacco-juice within a yard of them."

explosives. Camps were established every two miles, with a meat packer named Pat Burns providing beef for the thousands of men. Animals were driven overland from Chilcotin and butchered at Hazelton, with meat delivered to construction camps by the *Skeena*. She hauled so much meat, in fact, that she became known as 'Pat Burns' boat.'

In 1910 the last sternwheeler joined the fleet. She was the *Inlander*, built in Victoria for a company formed largely of Skeena River businessmen and residents. She was described as "not much to look at for shape, but good for fast water." She arrived at Hazelton on her first trip in June, 1910, and immediately started earning a very satisfactory profit. But the Skeena section of the railway was nearing completion, and for the sternwheelers, time was waving goodbye.

A month earler the *Omineca Herald* noted: "Another season of navigation has opened . . . the twentieth since steamboating commenced on the Skeena and the last in which our freight will be brought from salt water in river steamers. Another year and railway construction will have advanced to a point where the boats will get their cargo at the end of the first hundred miles from Prince Rupert."

In September 1912 the newspaper's prophecy came true. The *Inlander* shouldered her bluff bow into the Skeena River at Hazelton. In minutes she had disappeared, leaving behind swirls of black smoke which rose high above the totem poles and a wake of foam soon absorbed by the river. As she dropped downstream she was sailing into history, for she was the last sternwheeler to leave Hazelton. On yet another waterway paddlewheelers had completed their job.

Of the vessels, the *Distributor*, *Operator* and *Conveyor* sailed down the coast to Victoria where they were dismantled. Machinery from the *Distributor* became part of a new vessel on the Mackenzie River, while that from *Operator* and *Conveyor* was installed in two new sternwheelers for the railway contractors at Tete Jaune Cache near the headwaters of the Fraser River. The *Skeena* sailed to Vancouver where she plied the Lower Fraser, while the *Omineca* headed north to Alaska to help build another railway. Fate of the *Hazelton* and the *Inlander* wasn't so romantic. The former was dismantled and her hull sold to the Prince Rupert Yacht Club, while the latter was pulled onto the ways at Port Essington and left to rot.

But even as the sternwheelers were fading into history, the railway they helped to build was dying. On April 15, 1912, its visionary president, Charles M. Hays, was one of 1,635 drowned in the *Titanic* disaster. He was last seen standing on the slanting deck of the doomed vessel, waving goodbye to the lifeboat carrying his wife and daughter.

Without his guidance, the G.T.P. withered. In 1912 the bankrupt line was taken over by the Federal Government to become part of the C.N.R. By then only the *Skeena* survived. She was still plying the Lower Fraser River, kept alive by the devotion of her skipper-owner, but soon to be scrapped. Pat Burns, the man who supplied the meat she once hauled, became the most successful of all those connected with rail construction. From a start in Manitoba with a cow bought on credit and sold for $4, he built one of the world's largest meat packing empires. Prince Rupert, the city that was to be the north-coastal metropolis, languished and only today is maturing into the key port which Hays visualized over a half century ago.

she reached Arrow Lakes, but ice had already formed. With temperature 28 below she unloaded her impatient passengers and returned to winter quarters.

Meanwhile, merchants in British Columbia and on Vancouver Island clamored for a direct route to Big Bend so that they could profit from supplying the area. As a consequence, in December, 1865, the Colonial Government awarded well-known roadbuilder G. B. Wright a contract to build a wagon road from Cache Creek to Savona's Ferry at the west end of Kamloops Lake. The Government also stated that a stern-wheeler would provide a link to Seymour City, a community which had sprouted at the head of Shuswap Lake, and that it would pay $400 a month operating subsidy. Among those who sought to provide the vessel were Captains Irving and Moore. The former was chosen but transferred his contract to the H.B.C. In February 1866, a crew arrived at William Chase's ranch on Little Shuswap Lake and started hand-sawing lumber for the vessel.

The impatient miners, meanwhile, couldn't wait. In March, 400 left New Westminster alone, but found both Kamloops and Shuswap Lakes frozen. Some 250 set out over the ice, dragging their gear on sleds. Others waited at Fort Kamloops and when ice finally broke, launched canoes, rafts, and a variety of homespun craft.

About the same time Captain White again swung his Forty-Nine into the Columbia, determined to "knock the Thompson River route into a cocked hat." With fare $25 a head and freight $200 a ton she loaded up, reaching the head of navigation at Death Rapids on April 26, 11 days from Colville. She landed 89 optimistic miners, but took aboard over 100. They denounced the Big Bend as a fake and said that a better name was "Big Bilk." On her second trip the Forty-Nine carried north 110 passengers and 40 tons of freight; on her third trip, three passengers.

While Captain White was learning that Big Bend couldn't support a sternwheeler, construction continued on the H.B.C. vessel. Meanwhile, canoes, rowboats, and scows plied the lake, with Captain William Moore operating two of the latter. On April 23, 1866, a British Colonist correspondent reported: "Captain Moore is the same energetic, hard-working man he was in Victoria. He has two boats, both scows, built, one of which is decked over for passengers, the other is intended for freight. . . ."

Scows and canoes, however, weren't popular. Wrote one traveller: ". . . took passage in a large canoe for Seymour and paid $10. There being eighteen men crowded in the boat there was anything but comfort in the crossing. We were obliged to paddle and pay as well."

At Chase's Ranch, meanwhile, carpenters had completed the hull and superstructure of the new sternwheeler. A problem was that the engines were at Savona, some 60 roadless miles away, so the vessel was floated and sailed down the Thompson River and across Kamloops Lake. By the third week of May she was almost completed. With her black hull, white superstructure and name in gold letters, the $63,000 vessel looked as sleek as the animal whose name she bore, the marten.

The Marten is "a credit to the Colony," wrote one reporter, "being not only an extremely nice model but well and substantially built besides."

At 5 o'clock on May 26 she left on her maiden voyage under Captain W. A. Mouatt, escorted by Indians who "rode furiously along the beach trying to keep up with her." She arrived at Fort Kamloops at 7:45 a.m., then left next morning at 6 a.m., arriving at Seymour City at 6 p.m.

On her arrival, a correspondent for the Victoria Colonist wrote: "Five hundred hungry pioneers about that time were partaking of their evening dose of beans and bacon, but at the sight of the steamer they hurriedly cast pots and panni-kins aside. . . . Every available explosive weapon was brought to bear so that the steamer might receive a hearty welcome. As she neared the landing place three rousing cheers and a tiger rent the air. . . ." Since Captain Mouatt had freely distributed rum and champagne to all on board during the trip, passengers and crew lustily responded to the welcome.

Seymour City, outfitting point for the journey over the Gold Range to Big Bend, then had among business places six saloons, five bakeries, eleven shoemakers, a drug store, a tin shop, eight washhouses, plus "two breweries, two blacksmith's shops and a livery stable, to say nothing of a coffee and doughnut stand."

Unfortunately for Seymour, Big Bend proved a failure. Official yield for 1865 was only $250,000, less than a single claim in Cariboo. Miners left the region, and among freight abandoned on the trail over Gold Range were slate slabs for two billiard tables. The Forty-Nine made her last trip November 15, most passengers travelling only because Captain White accepted their I.O.U.'s. The Marten was tied up at Savona, then later brought to the H.B.C. post at Kamloops.

Among those to leave was Captain William Moore, even though he had pre-empted land 12 miles from Fort Kamloops and built a house. He loaded family and household goods into two wagons and headed up the Cariboo Wagon Road to Barkerville. But not all miners left. Some liked the lake-studded, semi-open Kamloops and Shuswap country and established farms and ranches.

By 1872 pioneer businessman John Adams felt there was enough freight for a steamer. Shortly afterwards he launched the Kamloops, a modest vessel with a one-man crew, Captain August Menenteau. For power the Kamloops used a four-horse engine originally installed in a flour mill at Soda Creek in 1867. Since the hand-me-down engine required most attention, Captain Menenteau ran lines to the wheel house and steered his vessel like a horse and buggy.

Despite this deficiency, on November 9, 1872, the New Westminster Mainland Guardian noted: ". . . she has proved quite a success; draws about 8 inches of water, and steams 12 knots an hour. She took a large and fashionable party of excursionists on Sunday last, from Savona's Ferry. She will prove a real boon to the farmers and traders in the vicinity."

In 1874 the Kamloops carried the first white woman settler up Spallumcheen River to north Okanagan. She was Mrs. A. L. Fortune. To emphasize the event, the Kamloops glided into Fortune's Landing with "whistle blowing and the Union Jack and Stars and Stripes flying."

Next year competition arrived. Businessmen J. A. Mara, F. J. Barnard, and W. B. Wilson purchased the Marten. She had been tied up at Fort Kamloops, a constant worry to H.B.C. clerk John Tait. In a letter May 30, 1874 he wrote to his superiors: "The steamer Marten is alright at present. She is pumped out occasionally. I find the greatest danger is when the ice is breaking up . . . on two occasions last spring we had great difficulty in keeping her afloat." On January

27, 1875, he reported ". . . I think she will be very apt to go down in spring". Then on February 8 Tait wrote, with obvious relief: "Your telegram arrived requesting me to deliver the steamer *Marten* to William B. Wilson . . . I did so on the 6th instant. And his receipt is herewith enclosed and am glad to say she is safe out of my hands."

Even though Tait felt that the *Marten* was "safe out of his hands," he wasn't free of her. Over the years her furniture had found its way into the house where Tait lived, and the new owners demanded it all back. A long and hot argument ensued. Then the vessel knocked down the entire east wing of a large H.B.C. warehouse at Savona. Tait was now ready for war, especially since he was also smarting from an attempt by Mara to force the H.B.C. to pay higher freight rates.

"Eight dollars a ton from Savona Ferry to Kamloops is outrageous," he heatedly wrote. He thereupon built a scow and the Bay did its own freighting. Now Mara was outraged. Fortunately, before warfare erupted the *Marten* distracted

him by slamming into a rock in Kamloops Lake. The accident happened, as Tate observed almost gleefully, "within 30 yds, I am told, of the shore, calm, and that beach well known by all."

The vessel was hauled ashore but found beyond repair. On July 11, 1879, she was offered for auction along with a "telegraph building plant, two trains of mules, and other supplies." Years later her rotting hulk was still on the beach.

Meanwhile, the *Kamloops* also reached the end of her days. In 1878 she was dismantled and her four-horse engine

Kamloops in 1885, with the Peerless, Kamloops and Spallumcheen at the steamboat landing. The Kamloops completed her first voyage in April, a newspaper account noting: "She made a fine appearance with her colors flying and moved along gracefully and fast against the current. The Kamloops will prove a great acquisition to our inland navigation. . . . The enterprising owners deserve, and very likely will receive, fair returns for outlay."

installed in a new vessel, the *Spallumcheen*. Built for the Kamloops Steam Navigation Company, she was to ply the Spallumcheen River some 25 miles from Shuswap Lake to Fortune's Landing. Since the river tends to be shallow—in places knee-deep water is virtually a flood—the *Spallumcheen* was built accordingly. At launching she floated in 3½ inches of water; with machinery and supplies aboard she required only 3 more. Her ancient engine worked satisfactorily, although it tended to clatter and thump, earning her the title "Noisy Peggy."

On October 15 another sidewheeler appeared. She was the *Lady Dufferin*, launched at Tranquille for William Fortune in the presence of people from all over the district. An observer for the *Victoria Daily Standard* recorded: "The *Lady Dufferin* is one of the most perfectly shaped little craft afloat in the Province. She is 90 feet in length, 16 feet beam, about 106 tons measurement, draws 9 inches of water."

On her trial trip December 2 the paper reported that ". . . with cheer after cheer, the new boat struck out into the placid waters of the lake, apparently as much at home in her new element as though she had been for years walking the waters."

At Kamloops she received a "royal salute whose echo rang for miles, startling the settlers in many a cabin." That evening residents welcomed the new arrival with a celebration that ended with ". . . the good people carrying Mr. Fortune from his boat through the town on a chair."

For two years the vessels were the only link for settlers along the lakes and rivers. But this condition changed with news that a trans-continental railway, the Canadian Pacific, was to be built to the Pacific Ocean. It would parallel Shuswap Lake and Thompson River, with Kamloops to be a divisional point. Once construction started and crews approached from both east and west, the district boomed.

To capitalize on activity, the Kamloops Steam Navigation Company, which now included famed Captain John Irving among its directors, ordered a new vessel. She was the *Peerless*, launched at Kamloops in November 1880. A few

The Lady Dufferin, *a vessel popular with pioneers of the Shuswap. One reason for a paddlewheeler's popularity was given in 1876 when the Earl of Dufferin, then Governor-General of Canada, visited B.C. and travelled from Savona to Kamloops on the* Marten. *Of the trip, Lady Dufferin wrote:*

"After passing through arid plains, we suddenly came upon a glassy sheet of water . . . We got on board a steamer, and as usual found every comfort and luxury surrounding us: pictures in our cabins; books of poetry on the tables; rocking-chairs; and good beds."

days later the *Victoria Colonist* reported: "The steamer *Peerless* . . . is as regards speed and draft, the most successful boat of her class yet built in the province."

She was 131 feet long, with 16 watertight compartments and powerful engines that drove her at 18 knots. With stores and fuel aboard, she required water only 18 inches deep. In June, 1881, she sailed over 100 miles up North Thompson River, then later that month ventured down the Thompson to Spences Bridge with flour for C.P.R. construction crews. On her return only Captain Irving's skill prevented her from being wrecked. She was five days fighting rocks and rapids in Black Canyon, a stretch of river considered among the most dangerous in the province.

In 1885 two more sternwheelers appeared. First was the *Kamloops*, far superior to her namesake. Aided by the traditional champagne launching, she "glided gracefully amid enthusiasm into the water of the Thompson."

Second vessel was the *Skuzzy*, built in a record 44 days for railway contractor A. Onderdonk and equipped with engines from the *Skuzzy* of Fraser Canyon fame. Her career was brief. She was used to deliver construction supplies from Savona along Kamloops and Shuswap Lakes to Eagle River. She served also as a floating mess-hall, following construction gangs and pulling ashore at meal times. But when the Kamloops-Shuswap section of C.P.R. was finished so was the *Skuzzy*.

Arrival of the first trans-continental train in Kamloops on November 7, 1885 ended the district's dependence on sternwheelers. For many years, however, they remained an essential transportation link. Rails served only a portion of Shuswap Lake's 600-mile shoreline. Farmers and ranchers on the north shore of Kamloops Lake and South Thompson River, as well as North Thompson and Spallumcheen Valleys, still depended on water transportation. Then, too, a growing lumber industry used sternwheelers extensively for hauling supplies and towing logs throughout the inland waterway. During the next 20 years, several new vessels appeared.

First was the *Queen*, built for J. E. Saucier, a man who appreciated publicity and who kept the local paper fully informed about his vessel. Readers, in fact, followed the *Queen* through construction, brief career, and fiery end.

On Saturday, April 14, 1894 the *Sentinel* reported that she would be "78 feet over all, 14 feet beam and 5 feet deep of hold, with the passenger deck above the main deck, and 18 inches depth of draft." Her boiler and machinery were from the *Lady Dufferin,* which had been removed from service a few years previously.

On May 16, 1894 the new vessel was launched in the "presence of quite a large gathering of citizens." A reporter noted that while she wasn't large, she was "a staunch, well-built vessel and will draw scarcely more than nine inches of water, when light." Her boiler was tested and "found most capable in every respect."

Regular news items in the *Sentinel* indicated that Saucier kept the *Queen* busy. She freighted cattle across the Thompson, hay and other farm produce up and downstream, and hauled bricks to Kamloops from up the North Thompson. Then, on July 6, 1894 she was again in the paper, this time with an ominous headline "DEATH AND DESTRUCTION."

At 7:30 a.m., July 4 the "most capable" boiler blew up, demolishing the vessel and killing her cook, Joseph Priette,

and a fireman, Joseph Rushond. Among those on board was owner J. E. Saucier, who became the first man to watch a boiler explode and live. He was lying on a mattress when he heard a noise like someone striking the boiler with a crowbar. He looked around quickly and saw the boiler shatter. The blast blew him out of the vessel and whirled him through the air like a rag. He landed in the lake, shaken and bruised, the mattress still beneath him. The *Sentinel* reported that: "He instinctively rubbed the soot and ashes from his eyes, and beheld a sight he could not describe. There were the bodies of the others just falling amid a shower of wood and debris of the boat. He was much excited and knew not what to do, but scrambled to get on the largest part of the boat he could see floating and to assist the other men."

An inquiry into the disaster revealed that the *Queen* was a somewhat loosely run vessel. Instead of the required 55 life preservers she carried 20, more or less; she was fitted with a lifeboat only on her second-to-last trip; her certificate limited her boiler to 75 pounds of steam, but Saucier ad-

The upper photo shows the Selkirk and above is the Skuzzy, built in a record 44 days to aid construction of the C.P.R. along the Shuswap-Kamloops waterway.

mitted seeing the gauge as high as 100. Captain Ritchie testified that he believed "the gauge and valves had been tampered with." The *Sentinel* was more forthright and stated: "The safety valve a plaything easily kept silent—many of the regulations not lived up to. . . ."

Sternwheel days, however, didn't die with the *Queen*. In 1895 appeared two new vessels, *Selkirk* and *Thompson*. Although neither was as newsworthy as the *Queen*, the *Selkirk* during a short career did provide some interesting copy.

She was built for H. C. Forster, a "capitalist who has decided to spend the summer in Kamloops and vicinity." She was 62 feet long with a single cabin 18 by 10 feet, and although described as "a beautiful model with fine lines," was top heavy.

She made her headlines June 29, 1898. About 25 miles above Kamloops she turned into a small eddy and suddenly capsized. Trapped in her main cabin were two women passengers, Mrs. Lemeriux and Mrs. Genier, and their eight

children. They were in grave peril since the vessel was still floating downstream but sinking, the cabin filling with water as she settled into the river. Only quick action and disregard for their own safety by Captain Forster, three crew members, and three male passengers saved the trapped group. They clambered up the side and broke into the cabin to rescue the soaking, terrified occupants. The vessel eventually stranded on a sandbar with the wet survivors taken ashore in a canoe.

The *Selkirk* was refloated three months later, then on her way downstream capsized again. She was righted a second time and safely tied up. By now her deckhouse had washed away, although she was otherwise practically intact. Next spring Captain Forster loaded her on two flatcars for transfer to Golden on the Upper Columbia River.

Now only two vessels remained, *Thompson* and *Ethel Ross*. The latter had been built in 1897 by Captain G. B. Ward, a shipbuilder and sailor from the Maritimes who had settled in Kamloops. Over the next decade new vessels ap-

peared, but they were primarily for the lumber industry.

Among them were *Riffle,* built in 1902 for the Lamb-Watson Lumber Company; *Florence Carlin* in 1906 for Columbia River Lumber Company; and *C. R. Lamb* in 1907 for Arrow Lakes Lumber Company. The latter was described as having "exceedingly pretty lines for a sternwheeler, and the builder, Captain Ward, deserves great credit. . . ."

It was Captain Ward and his two sons, Elmer and Arthur, who tried to delay the inevitable day when sternwheelers would no longer ply Kamloops-Shuswap waterways. In

May, 1908, they launched the *Silver Stream,* but she wasn't profitable, despite a $1,500 government subsidy. In 1910 when Captain Ward was unable to get a further subsidy, he sold her to the Arrow Lakes Lumber Company.

Meanwhile, in 1909 the *A. R. Hellen* had been launched for Adams River Lumber Company, and later, the *Crombie* for the same firm. In 1912 the last vessel appeared. She was the *Distributor,* a 143-foot-long sternwheeler built to aid construction of the Canadian Northern Railway, a line that paralleled the North Thompson and Thompson Rivers on

---

On the opposite page pioneer residents enjoy an excursion on the Forest Stream and the Thompson. Excursions were popular and often eventful. On one trip on Kamloops Lake band music blew overboard and the voyage was temporarily delayed while a boat was launched to recover the music. On another a daring young blade released a mouse among the ladies "which caused quite a panic."

One correspondent boarded a sternwheeler which was tak-

ing the Kamloops lacrosse team to Savona for a game with Ashcroft. The steamer had a scow lashed alongside for dancing but just before she set out "two kegs were rolled on board. I thought at the time that probably they contained oatmeal water or some other mild refreshment for the lacrosse boys, but later on found out my mistake."

At lower left is the Ethel Ross; below, the Florence Carlin; at bottom the Distributor being launched in 1912.

its route from Eastern Canada to Vancouver. Like *Skuzzy* over 25 years before, the *Distributor* carried powder, rails, and supplies for construction crews. When the railway was completed her machinery was removed and hull abandoned near Sicamous.

One by one the remaining vessels joined her. The hull of the *Florence Carlin* was abandoned near Salmon Arm; *A. R. Hellen* on Adams Lake; *Peerless, Skuzzy, Kamloops* and others fell apart or burned at Kamloops; while part of the *Andover*, formerly *Silver Stream*, became a summer cottage on Paul Lake. Finally only the *C. R. Lamb* remained.

She was apparently slated to join the others in decay but in January 1933 was purchased by Captain William Louie, a local businessman of Chinese descent. Soon after the Victoria *Daily Colonist* carried a front page headline: "REBUILDING BRIDGE THAT CHINESE MAY MARKET POTATOES." The item went on: "Louie sat one day at Shuswap Lake, contemplating his large supplies of potatoes, some piles of cordwood and some river boats that have been tied up at a dock since the early days. After a while, the potatoes, the cordwood and the river boats merged in Louie's mind into a great plan. He would buy one of the boats, load it with potatoes and cordwood and ship them to market at Kamloops much more cheaply than by rail. Then he would ship other people's products back and forth and do well for himself."

In reply Captain Louie pointed out that since he had been born, brought up, and educated in Canada, he had fair reason to consider himself Canadian. Furthermore, he didn't own or grow potatoes and if he did it wouldn't make much sense carrying them from Chase to Kamloops. He went on to state that the *C. R. Lamb* was thoroughly overhauled and that he intended to run her between Kamloops and Shuswap Lake. He had operated boats on the system and "have a good idea of what business can be done by a boat on this run."

He added that when the bridge does have a lift span "the settlers and residents along the South Thompson River and

At right is the *A. R. Hellen* in 1909 with the second tow of logs to arrive at the foot of Adams Lake. The men in the rowboat turned the logs loose so that they ran Lower Adams River to Shuswap Lake.

Passengers on a sternwheeler towing a log boom experienced a slow journey as English author Morley Roberts discovered when he boarded the Peerless at Eagle Pass Landing. He wrote in his book The Western Avernus: "We had reckoned on being in Savona's Ferry, about a hundred miles away, the next day, but we were doomed to disappointment for, instead of going direct to Kamloops . . . the boat . . . picked up a big 'boom of logs,' which she was to tow down to the sawmill at Kamloops. So, instead of going down flying, we had

to crawl along, doing about three miles an hour.

"My life on board those three days was commonplace and quiet. I slept and smoked and ate my bread and deer-meat, and at times talked with some of the deck hands, who were full Indians or half-breeds."

Above is the C. R. Lamb, with Captain William Louie and his cook on deck. For 25 years Captain Louie operated the C. R. Lamb, last of the sternwheelers. Throughout his lifetime he served Kamloops and District foremost. He was 23 years on the Kamloops Board of Trade plus being active in Rotary, on the school board, and other community organizations. He died March 22, 1956, severing the last link with Kamloops-Shuswap paddlewheel days

Shuswap Lake covering a shoreline of over three hundred miles will then regain this valuable outlet by water which has been used for over fifty years and their connection with the old port of Kamloops, their only port with two railways, and with its shipping firms, packing houses, canneries, factories and other business concerns."

The bridge problem arose when Captain Louie bought the *C. R. Lamb* from the Shuswap Transportation Company. By then the provincial government, certain that sternwheel days were over, had bridged the South Thompson at Pritchard. However, the river was still classed as navigable. Confronted with Captain Louie's plan, the government had to slice a chunk out of the bridge and "with a substantial expenditure" rebuild it with a lift span.

For many years Captain Louie sailed the *C. R. Lamb* from Enderby on Spallumcheen River to Savona on Kamloops Lake. He carried cordwood, hay, potatoes, excursion parties, and anything else offered. But, as time passed, more and more roads appeared. Eventually, the vessel was used

mostly for hauling cordwood from Shuswap Lake to Kamloops where Captain Louie operated a fuel business along with a service station. Finally in 1948 the *C. R. Lamb* was beached near Kamloops.

Her hull, filled with mud, is still on the river bank at the foot of 8th Ave., while preserved in the Kamloops Museum are a few remnants: her anchor, whistle, signal bell, helm, running lights, and life belt, plus Captain Louie's master's certificate, and a model built by S. B. Brooke. Perhaps some day they will be joined by another memento—the slate slabs intended for billiard tables at the Big Bend gold field. They are still on the pass where they were abandoned over a century ago.

Together with the bridge at Pritchard which still has its lift span and pieces of the *C. R. Lamb,* they are the reminders of an era that lasted about a lifetime. But it was an eventful lifetime. During it high-rise cities grew where stood miners' shacks and fur-trade forts, while jet planes replaced voyageurs' canoes and pioneering sternwheelers.

CHAPTER SEVEN

The Okanagan Valley

Compared with the rousing decades that characterized sternwheel activity on many B.C. lakes and rivers, the 43-year era on Okanagan waters was as peaceful as the yellow bells, blue lupine, and other wild flowers which decorate the Valley in spring. Missing were frenzied miners pursuing golden rainbows, ruinous competition, and boiler eruptions. A couple of sternwheelers did burn up, but with a minimum of fuss and no loss of life. This subdued atmosphere blended well with that of a region to become famous for sandy beaches, blue waters, and miles of apples, pears, peaches, and cherries maturing under sunny skies.

Possibly the nearest thing to an explosion occurred during the early 1900's when the C.P.R. sternwheeler *Aberdeen* brought some Doukhobors to settle around Penticton. Local residents refused to let them ashore. The Captain protested, pointing out with reasonable logic that he had orders to land the settlers. Townspeople, massed along the waterfront, shouted that they didn't care a hoot about orders. No Douks were landing and that was that. The Captain scanned the hostile crowd, at the same time mentally reviewing his orders. He decided that they didn't cover the situation and chuffed back to Okanagan Landing. Here his somewhat bewildered cargo was unloaded and shipped elsewhere.

A few years previously the sternwheeler *Red Star* had also caused a commotion when she freighted the first keg of rum up Spallumcheen River for delivery into the Valley. When the new arrival reached its destination at Lumby estate, a group of old-timers gathered to pay their respects. During the welcoming ritual, lightning seared a brown path through the evergreens on a nearby mountain. When peace returned an Indian summed up the incident with the observation: "I think God above must be really angry today!"

Steamboat days on Okanagan Lake began modestly on April 21, 1886. That day a 32-foot-long, 5-foot-wide vessel was launched at a point to be known as Okanagan Landing. She was the *Mary Victoria Greenhow*, a name, according to one joker, "almost as long as her hull." She wasn't a sternwheeler, but she was the first steam-powered vessel on the lake, even though her engine developed only two horse-

The Sicamous, "great white swan of Okanagan Lake." Many Okanagan place names originated during sternwheel days. Calling points were usually named after pioneer settlers— Ewing's Landing, Carr's Landing, Caesar's Landing, and Wilson's Landing are a few examples.

89

power. Her owner was Thomas Dolman Shorts, probably Okanagan's most colorful character.

He arrived about 1883 and pre-empted land on the west bank near the northern end of the lake. Previously he had operated a sawmill, run a fish market in California, sold needles on a street corner in Philadelphia, and mined in Cassiar. He soon decided that he didn't like farming so whip-sawed lumber and built a 22-foot rowboat. Then he started rowing up and down 69-mile-long Okanagan Lake.

A trip with Shorts was never speedy; on the other hand it was never dull. He rowed during the day and camped under a tree at night. Passengers who liked privacy found a tree of their own, otherwise all shared the same one. A round trip usually took three weeks, but the schedule was variable. Shorts hated routine. If a passenger asked how long a trip would take the answer was: "Haven't got the faintest idea, but rest assured we'll fetch up there sometime!"

When a storm blew up Shorts immediately headed for shore, commenting, "Shorts wasn't born to be drowned." On those few occasions when he was caught, he would toss out his anchor and comment: "There, Captain Shorts has done his duty, now let Providence look after the rest."

On her maiden voyage to Penticton his *Mary Victoria Greenhow* was laden to capacity—five tons of freight plus five passengers, tucked where convenient. All went well for a time, then the power plant stopped. Shorts had under-estimated fuel consumption. With typical forthrightness he got out his oars and rowed to the nearest settler. After borrowing the man's supply of lamp oil he again set sail. Thereafter, darkened windows recorded his progress as he alternately chugged and rowed from settler to settler, borrowing oil as he went.

At Penticton a 21-gun salute welcomed him, but since cannon were scarce, shotguns were substituted. After acknowledging the salute and borrowing more oil, Shorts resumed operations. Unfortunately, the *Mary Victoria Greenhow* caught fire at Okanagan Mission while he was busy borrowing oil. She was badly damaged, an experience that convinced Shorts wood was more practical than oil, besides being easier to obtain. The only problem was that he couldn't persuade his engine to switch diets. Thereupon he removed it, made some revisions, and put it into a new hull which he christened *Jubilee*.

The *Jubilee* operated successfully on wooden rations, although Shorts still had fuel problems. To meet any crisis he stockpiled wood all along the lake. On one trip, however, he ran out of fuel and had to burn part of his cargo of shakes to reach shore. The *Jubilee* plied the lake until December, 1889, when she was frozen in at Okanagan Landing. In spring when the ice thawed, she promptly sank.

Shorts, however, wasn't unduly concerned. During the winter he persuaded pioneer rancher Tom Ellis to invest in his steamship venture. In April, construction started on a new vessel, considerably larger than any previous unit of his fleet.

To maintain service during construction, Shorts salvaged the *Jubilee's* engine and installed it in another vessel optimistically called *City of Vernon*. She resembled "an open-deck scow with an engine," said one person. Another described her as "a little tub of very doubtful safety. . ." Despite these uncomplimentary remarks, the *City of Vernon* maintained a semblance of service until the new vessel appeared.

She was the *Penticton*, and while she was far larger than any of Shorts' previous vessels, her accommodation wasn't unduly lavish. She had only one cabin, furnished with one chair, available on a first-come, first-seated basis. Shorts didn't believe in pampering his passengers. Nor did he believe in punctuality. He hated routine, a trait which caused the *Penticton* to operate on a schedule described charitably as "semi-occasionally."

With the appearance of the *Penticton*, Shorts sold the *City of Vernon*. Her new owners soon nicknamed her the *Mud Hen* since she spent more time on the bottom than carrying cargo. They unloaded her on two Englishmen who salvaged the engine, built a new hull and mated the pair under the name *Wanderer*. She freighted for a number of years but was sold again and operated as the *Violet*. She is notable only in that the engine, the original two-horsepower, coal-oil powered plant which kept Shorts busy borrowing oil and settlers in darkness, is today on display at Vernon's museum.

At the time of Shorts' maritime activities, Okanagan was famous not for fruit but for ranches. Pioneers such as Judge

Captain T. D. Shorts, "a very likeable man, always genial and friendly." Nothing bothered him, except possibly one trip when his cargo included several kegs of whiskey owned by a farmer. The farmer came aboard carrying a sheaf of wheat, promptly bored a hole in one of the kegs and with a straw plucked from his sheaf, sampled the contents. All hands reached their destination safely, although the farmer was somewhat unsteady.

Captain Shorts rowed Okanagan Lake for three years, making $6,000 which he lost when he ventured into steam. He summed up his loss in a typically forthright manner: "Boys, if we only had as good foresight as we have hindsight, we would raise hell, wouldn't we." He left Okanagan for the Klondike gold rush and never returned. On February 9, 1921, he died at Hope, aged 84. The colorful individualist is commemorated by Shorts Creek, a tributary of Okanagan Lake.

Haynes, Theodore Kruger, Tom Ellis, Thomas Ward, Cornelius O'Keefe, and Thomas Greenhow held large acreage extending to the U.S. border. First permanent settlers were Fathers Pandosy and Richard who in 1860 built a house, school, and church near present-day Kelowna. Next year Mr. and Mrs. Eli Lequime arrived, their possessions on a horse, their two sons riding the family cow. Near the Mission they opened a general store and hotel, but were so isolated that supplies were eight days coming over the Dewdney Trail from Hope.

In those days only the country from the north end of Okanagan Lake past Dog Lake to the border was considered the Okanagan. The region between Okanagan Lake and Shuswap Lake was called Spallumcheen. In later years, however, names were somewhat changed. Dog Lake became Skaha Lake, while to the disgust of old-timers, Okanagan Valley became the entire area south of Shuswap Lake, and the Spallumcheen River became the Shuswap. It was this latter stream that felt the first throb of paddlewheeler in the Okanagan.

In the 1870's sternwheelers from Kamloops plied to the head of navigation at what is now Enderby. In 1888 appeared the first sternwheeler built especially for the Spallumcheen. She was the *Red Star*, built for R. P. Rithet to carry his "Moffat's Best" flour from his mill at Enderby to the C.P.R. mainline at Sicamous.

The *Red Star* was a nonchalant craft which would have delighted Captain Shorts. She ran, according to one description, "at irregular hours, carrying . . . such passengers as were in no hurry." Old-timers called her "Slow Molasses," while a *Vernon News* correspondent noted in June, 1891 that: "When steamships of the *Red Star* type have to be utilized in the mail service, we cannot always look for punctuality. . . ." One trip her captain, D. G. Cumming, didn't bother waiting for the mail at Sicamous. The mailman was

The Red Star *on the Spallumcheen River. To pioneers, sternwheelers were an important part of community life. People walked 2 and 3 miles to greet an arriving vessel, with the wharf becoming a meeting place for friends.*

understandably annoyed. But he was also resourceful. He borrowed a rowboat, then a saddle horse, and arrived at Enderby about the same time as the *Red Star*.

A trip up the 30 miles of river between Sicamous and Enderby took about 10 hours, if passengers were lucky. To prevent the trip becoming monotonous, Captain Cumming related stories about people and places along the way, and added a picnic flavor by serving meals on deck if mosquitoes weren't too bad.

While the *Red Star* was no greyhound, she provided a useful service. Then in 1890 construction started on a railway from Sicamous to Okanagan Landing, and its completion early in 1892 ended the *Red Star's* service. She was abandoned at Enderby, eventually broken up by spring floods and washed downstream.

The new railway, operated under lease by the C.P.R., assured northern Okanagan of its first reliable transportation. Okanagan Lake itself was still a problem since Captain Shorts' one-ship fleet hadn't grown. The C.P.R. looked things

over and in December 1892 started building a sternwheel steamer to serve the lake. The decision changed the economy of the entire Okanagan.

Spurred by prospect of a reliable transportation system, land speculators bought ranches and sub-divided them into orchard plots. Then in newspaper advertisements they

---

Okanagan Lake. When regular service was established on the lake there were 19 calls on the West Shore and 9 on the East. Anyone, however, was privileged to call a sternwheeler ashore. A recognized signal was a white cloth, shirt or other garment, or two fires on the beach.

On Okanagan Lake sternwheelers, farm- and orchard-fresh produce was a feature of meals. For many years Mrs. R. Munson, one of the first white women in the Kelowna district, supplied the Aberdeen, then the Okanagan, with butter, cream, and eggs.

As one traveller wrote: "The meals were of the best, with charge for all one could eat seventy-five cents."

pointed out the delights of fruit growing. Orchardists more or less sat in the shade, they hinted, while fruit grew ripe and profitable. The advertisements attracted world-wide interest, and soon settlers from many nations were heading to Okanagan.

Meanwhile, at Okanagan Landing the new sternwheeler took shape. On May 3, 1893 she was ready to launch. People crowded Okanagan Landing from all over the Valley, while the mayor of Vernon even declared a half-day holiday. The editor of the *Vernon News* was so impressed that he resorted to both poetry and prose to report the launching.

One stanza urged:
"Then strike away the bars and blocks
And set the good ship free;
While lingers on these dusty rocks
The Young Bride of the Sea?"
As the editor waited for the actual launch he noted that,
"Day by day the vessel grew,
With timbers fashioned strong and true."

As the time neared he informed readers that she was,
"Still at rest on sandy beach
Just beyond the billows reach."
Finally, workmen were ready and ". . . she started slowly and smoothly down the ways gathering velocity as 'the thrill of life was felt along its keel' and before they had time to realize what fully was happening, the *Aberdeen* was riding out proudly on the water."

Pioneer residents accustomed to Captain Shorts' varied vessels were amazed at the size and furnishings of the *Aberdeen*. Her gross tonnage was ten times that of any pre-

Launching of the Aberdeen and the vessel under full steam. The Aberdeen left Okanagan Landing on Monday, Wednesday and Friday after arrival of the train at 10:30, reached Kelowna at 1:00 p.m. and Penticton about 4:30 p.m. On the return voyage she left Penticton at noon the following day, reaching Kelowna about 3:00 p.m. and Okanagan Landing in time to connect with the train for Sicamous.

vious vessel. Instead of one cabin with one chair like the *Penticton,* she had an observation lounge with plush seats, red carpet, and curtains. She had a promenade deck, a bar to be opened if passengers requested, a dining room complete with white tablecloth and stewards. Her staterooms had white sheets on the beds, even screens to keep out mosquitoes. In addition to these luxuries, she could carry 200 tons of freight, undercover at that. More remarkable, she would be able to travel the entire lake in less than a day.

One man unimpressed by the excitement was Captain Thomas Dolman Shorts. He summed up his feelings in a newspaper advertisement which noted: "The opposition is here to stay, and so am I."

At the time he was temporarily without a vessel, but the optimistic Shorts solved this hurdle. He acquired an old hulk, renamed her *Lucy* and set forth to challenge "that grasping octopus of a C.P.R." The result was predictable. Before long he was again boatless.

The *Aberdeen* began scheduled service early in June. She left Okanagan Landing on Monday, Wednesday, and Friday, docked at Penticton overnight, then returned next day. A trip took about six hours, depending on calls. At many points there were no wharf facilities. At these places she simply nosed into the beach, stopping to deliver a package to an isolated settler as readily as if she were getting a full cargo. As C.P.R. divisional superintendent R. Marpole emphasized, the boat was built "not for sentiment, but for business."

At first business wasn't too plentiful, then after 1897 she operated to capacity. Mineral development in the Kettle Valley, Southern Okanagan, and Similkameen created a host of thriving communities: Midway, Greenwood, Grand Forks, Fairview, Hedley, and similar settlements. Passengers and freight arrived at Penticton on the *Aberdeen* then continued by stagecoach or freight wagon. In addition, Peachland,

At bottom left is Kelowna about 1905 and at bottom right Penticton's waterfront in 1907. Lower left shows Okanagan Landing in 1904 and, below, Vernon in 1890.

Summerland, and other lakeside communities appeared. To them the sternwheeler brought settlers and their effects, plus tens of thousands of fruit trees for benchland orchards.

During 1901 the vessel helped ship the first carload of Okanagan apples to market. For two weeks she patiently gathered 700 boxes from around the lake—birth of an industry that grew from the modest 700 boxes annually to some 10,000,000.

During her career, the *Aberdeen* experienced some competition, although it carried a homespun flavor. In 1894 the sternwheeler *Fairview* appeared. She was 55-feet long by 15 wide, with a single passenger cabin 13 by 18 feet and a three-man crew: captain, engineer, and deckboy. She was designed to ply the 12-mile section of Okanagan River between Okanagan and Dog Lakes, but since the river was somewhat narrow and shallow, there were problems. On one trip there was a delay when a snag plucked off part of her sternwheel and rudder. Most memorable voyage, however, was when a tree ripped into the pilothouse and knocked her captain overboard.

These episodes, together with pushing and prying her off sandbars, proved somewhat discouraging. Consequently, she served mostly on Okanagan Lake. Once she delivered to Kelowna some American settlers who trekked to Okanagan in covered wagons from Idaho. Frequently she was chartered to carry baseball, cricket and other teams. On one such trip on July 2, 1897 she caught fire at Okanagan Landing and burned up while her crew were enjoying a thirst quencher at the local hotel.

Replacing the *Fairview* was another privately-owned sternwheeler, the *Greenwood*. Although she could sail in water only knee deep, she also had problems on Okanagan River and was used mostly on the lake. Her career, however, was short. In 1899 she burned at Okanagan Falls.

During the early 1900's Okanagan expansion accelerated as advertising continued to attract settlers. More ranches became orchards, including Tom Ellis' pioneer spread at Penticton, bought for $400,000 and sub-divided by the Southern Okanagan Land Company. To cope with traffic, in April 1907 the C.P.R. launched another sternwheeler, the *Okanagan*.

She was larger and faster than the *Aberdeen*, could carry 250 passengers, and was elaborately fitted out. One paper reported: "On the main deck the ladies' and gentlemen's cabins are large and airy apartments, finished in gold and enamel and furnished in a style that leaves nothing to be desired. . . . the dining room, adorned with a handsome sideboard of Australian cedar at one end, and an elegant mirror at the other, is large and roomy."

On June 6, 1907, she started a six-times-a-week express service from Okanagan Landing to Penticton and back, with calls at Summerland, Peachland, and Kelowna. The *Aberdeen* continued her three-trips-a-week schedule, with stops at all way points.

In 1910 another sternwheeler, the *Kaleden,* joined the C.P.R. fleet. Although she wasn't big, 94-feet long by 18 wide, she proved more embarrassing to the company than any other vessel they owned. In fact, old-timers still remember her with a chuckle of satisfaction.

She was intended to serve between Okanagan and Dog Lakes on Okanagan River, despite the unhappy experiences of *Fairview* and *Greenwood* on that waterway. The river,

however, had been dredged and cleared of snags. This improvement made Captain J. C. Gore, superintendent of the C.P.R.'s lake fleet, feel that sternwheeler service was now practical.

On her maiden voyage the *Kaleden* had two captains aboard, D. C. McMorris in command, J. C. Gore as confident observer. Within minutes, the captains' composure and confidence were a shambles. Although the vessel could sail in water a bathtub deep, there just wasn't that depth in the river. Consequently, the *Kaleden* performed like a young billy goat. She smacked sandbars left and right, thumped into mudbanks, butted one shore then the other. At one point she jammed completely sideways; a miniature dam, bow overlooking one bank, stern the other.

Her perspiring crew pulled, pried, kicked, and shoved her downstream; then slaved even harder on the trip back

Launching the Okanagan *in April 1907 and, below, the rambunctious* Kaleden *at Okanagan Landing.*

against the current. In all, the 12-mile downstream trip took three days; the return, a week. News of the unique voyage circulated throughout the Okanagan and beyond. Each repetition added to the humor. The cruise became known as "Gore's Gaff" and was the first and last trip on Okanagan River for both Captain Gore and *Kaleden*. Thereafter she was used exclusively on Okanagan Lake.

On the lake she served chiefly as a freighter, her most useful service carrying tons of blasting powder for construction of the Kettle Valley Railway. This line, a C.P.R. subsidiary, was to link the Kootenays, Kettle Valley, and Southern Okanagan to Vancouver via Penticton and Hope. It also brought the first chill of evening to Okanagan sternwheel days.

By 1911, construction was well underway. Penticton became the major supply point and it boomed. Land which sold a few years before for $1 an acre now brought $1,000. In 1912 there were 22 real estate firms in the community, most of them sub-dividing ranches into orchard plots.

Next year, the *Aberdeen* completed 20 years of service. During her years on the lake, a generation grew up. Young couples who strolled hand in hand during her first moonlight excursions were grandparents; babies once rocked to sleep as she throbbed down the lake were adults with families of their own; and settlements that she helped establish—Penticton, Kelowna, Naramata, Summerland, Peachland, and many others—were becoming major communities. She was ready for retirement, although to Valley residents parting would be like losing one of the family.

In 1914 a lusty replacement slid into the water at Okanagan Landing. She was the $180,000 *Sicamous,* one of the largest sternwheelers to appear in B.C. Her steel hull was divided into 20 watertight compartments and she could carry upward of 500 passengers plus freight at a speed of 17 knots.

The vessel became the showpiece of the Okanagan, still remembered with pride by old-timers. Staterooms and furnishings were finished in B.C. cedar, Douglas fir, Australian mahogany, and Burmese teak. Hardware fittings were brass

imported from Scotland. Her skylights were a rainbow of color, while plate glass mirrors sparkled everywhere. At bow and stern enclosed observation and smoking lounges presented a panoramic view of bountiful orchards and blue water, green-clad hills and yellow sand beaches. Her 65-foot-long dining room with spotless linen, excellent food and service became famous far beyond the Valley. She soon won the title "Queen of Okanagan Lake."

On her maiden voyage throngs of people welcomed her at

Workmen pose as the Sicamous, complete with flags flying, waits to be launched. At opposite left is the Okanagan. In contrast to the spartan facilities offered travellers by most early-day Okanagan stopping places, accommodation on even the first sternwheelers was tops. For instance in 1893 the Vernon News reported that on the Aberdeen there are "11 cozy staterooms for the accommodation of passengers, and the bedding is all of a very expensive class, while ventilation is well attended to. . . ."

every community, but shortly after she entered service, a somber attitude replaced the gaiety. The First World War erupted. Her decks were soon jammed with men on their way overseas, including the entire Penticton band. Later her shrill whistle summoned residents to help a wounded veteran ashore or receive sad news about a son or husband.

During the war so many men enlisted that expansion in the Valley stopped. Then the fruit boom collapsed and freight shipments decreased. Completion of the Kettle Valley Railway in 1916 further depleted business. The *Aberdeen, Okanagan,* and *Kaleden* were laid up. Only *Sicamous* remained in service, maintaining her six-times-a-week service. A notable exception was 1916 when the lake froze. She smashed a path in deep water but for weeks could not dock at Penticton. Her crew made deliveries to many communities by sled, and on the lake amused themselves by skating alongside as she crunched through the ice.

By her tenth birthday, the *Sicamous* was a landmark, familiar and popular as cherry blossoms in spring. Okana-

gan historian Eric Sismey noted: " . . . she served much more than the needs of growing communities and those of the lonely settler. In early years, when two weeks' vacation had not become the rule, a round trip on the sternwheeler was often as much a holiday as we could manage, and a more enjoyable outing would be hard to find: blue sky, blue water, and the cool breeze of a summer's day . . . farmsteads and young orchards along the shore, backdropped by grey-green hills . . . friendly talk with fellow passengers . . . a picnic basket on the upper deck . . . lunch and dinner in the dining saloon chosen from a menu the size of this page. . . ."

Unfortunately, the *Sicamous* was being outmoded by trucks, buses and cars which cut ever deeper into her freight and passenger trade. Then on February 15, 1926 the C.N.R. completed a spur line between Kamloops and Kelowna. There was another drop in business, with the result inevitable. In April 1931, the C.P.R. terminated sternwheel service on Okanagan Lake.

Boards of Trade vigorously protested, and the *Sicamous* was reprieved for a few more years. Finally, on January 5,

1935, she was tied up at Okanagan Landing. In an attempt to reduce operating costs she was shorn of top deck and other superstructure but used only during the 1935 and 1936 fruit-shipping season. Her last trip with passengers was 1936 when the Penticton Gyro Club chartered her for an excursion.

Meanwhile, the other sternwheelers disappeared. The *Aberdeen*, a summer home for many years, was finally dismantled. *Kaleden* was scrapped at Okanagan Landing in 1918, her hull became a breakwater for Captain J. North; her housework, a garage for Captain J. B. Weeks. *Okanagan* was scrapped in 1937, parts of her woodwork became summer cabins, her boiler used in a Kelowna cannery. *Sicamous* seemed likely to join them in oblivion.

For 16 years she lay at Okanagan Landing, buffeted by winter gales, baked by the summer sun—a queen without a throne. Then the Penticton Gyro Club became interested. They spearheaded a campaign that resulted in the C.P.R. selling her for $1 and the city of Penticton agreeing to build a permanent mooring place.

At far right is the massive sternwheel of the Sicamous. The "lawnmower," as it was nicknamed, is 24 feet in diameter. The vessel is permanently moored at the west end of Lakeshore Drive in Penticton.

Captain George Ludlow Estabrooks, above, was well known to all Okanagan pioneers. He started his career in 1890 with the Columbia-Kootenay Steam Navigation Company on the Arrow Lakes. On Okanagan Lake he commanded both the Okanagan and Sicamous on their maiden voyages.

Best known of all Okanagan captains was J. B. Weeks. In 1897 he joined the Aberdeen as a deckhand and by 1904 was in command of the York, a propeller-driven craft that served as a utility boat on Okanagan Lake. In 1907 he was promoted to captain of the Aberdeen and from 1922 to 1935 was captain of the Sicamous. Captain "Joe" was superannuated in 1942 after 45 years of service on inland waters. He died February 23, 1969 at 92, with his ashes scattered over the lake on which he had logged some 2 million miles.

On a rainy August 30, 1951, a tug towed her to Penticton. The *Penticton Herald* devoted most of its front page to the arrival: "Like a tired but proud old lady, the still seaworthy *Sicamous* . . . came home on Monday to her final resting place.

"Hundreds of Penticton people left homes and offices to extend to the famous sternwheeler the welcome she deserved. They lined the beach as the *Sicamous* moved slowly into shore, arousing pleasant nostalgia in the hearts of pioneers who saw vivid pictures of the old lake steamer plying Okanagan Lake. . . .

"The *Sicamous* was rather like an aged relative, timidly and shyly venturing into a final home, concerned as to whether there would really be a welcome, and finally settling down with relief when the whole business of the arrival was over."

Today she is one of only two sternwheelers preserved in B.C. No longer do her decks vibrate to the throb of her 19-foot-high sternwheel; no longer do handcarts clatter as deckhands wheel aboard boxes of sun-ripened fruit; no longer does her whistle blast speed over the whitecaps to echo from the mountains. Instead she is a museum, moored near Penticton's city center close to the Okanagan River where the *Kaleden* started her inglorious journey.

In summer, visitors roam her passageways, and children, looking at the empty pilothouse, sail an imaginary course over ripples to the timbered horizon. In winter, snow sifts around her bluff bow, ice levers against her hull, and north winds moan past rigging and funnel. Her paddlewheel and decks are silent and still. At times she seems lonely. She still, though, wears the proud look of a queen, facing squarely into the lake she knew so well and served so long.

Her era was summed up by veteran Okanagan Captain J. B. Weeks who wrote: "When sternwheelers were withdrawn, the comfort and joy of water travel enjoyed by the people along the shore of Okanagan Lake for half a century passed into history. The dawn of a speed-mad age had stolen much of the joy and the peace and the beauty from the very life of the lake—things that can never be replaced by bus or car, train or plane."

CHAPTER EIGHT

Columbia and Kootenay Rivers

She was "a pretty crude steamboat." Thus Captain F. P. Armstrong summed up the *Duchess*, first sternwheeler to ply the Upper Columbia River. Since Captain Armstrong built and owned her, his description was undoubtedly accurate.

Launched at Golden in 1886, the *Duchess* had an abandoned-barn appearance that even a royal name couldn't disguise. But considering her origin, the wonder wasn't that she was "slab-sided" with an "immense superstructure" but that she appeared at all. The lumber her 27-year-old captain used was the first problem. It was salvaged from an abandoned sawmill, a variety of widths, lengths and thicknesses. Because of this mismatched material Armstrong could follow no formal design. He fitted the odds and ends together as best he could and somehow a 74-foot-long hull evolved. Then he capped the lot with an upperworks that resembled an outhouse hit by a hurricane. As might be suspected, accommodation wasn't first class. The dining saloon was a table on the uneven deck while passengers who spent the night on board slept where they found space.

Below deck she was equally unpretentious. Her engines, for instance, had already worked nearly half a century in a ferry across the St. Lawrence River. When they came West they weren't in the best of shape, but then as Captain Armstrong admitted, neither was his vessel. Supporting this candid opinion was a delegation of Indians sent from Lake Windermere to inspect the new wonder. They even noticed a defect that Captain Armstrong had overlooked. "She was," they pronounced, "too big and too clumsy to be handled by oars."

Nevertheless in June the *Duchess* started up the Columbia, a shallow, winding waterway described as: "Such a variety of sand and mud banks, such an array of snags . . . has never been seen." The snags Captain Armstrong avoided, although in forthcoming years other skippers weren't so fortunate.

On his maiden voyage, though, the Captain did discover that in many places "the river's bottom was very close to the river's top." Among the many places where the *Duchess* grounded was the outlet of Lake Windermere. Here spawn-

The Nowitka on the Upper Columbia River with a barge load of construction supplies. The last sternwheeler to ply the Upper Columbia River, she made her final voyage in May 1920 commanded by Captain F. P. Armstrong, a famous Kootenay pioneer who opened the sternwheel era in 1886.

101

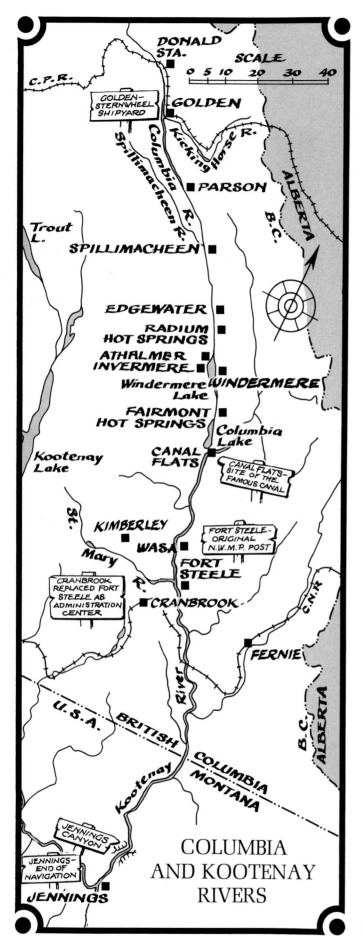

COLUMBIA AND KOOTENAY RIVERS

ing salmon left the bed in a series of gravel ridges, and on them the *Duchess* parked. For Captain Armstrong this mishap was the worst for here lived the Indians who had predicted that his vessel was too clumsy to be handled by oars. But instead of laughing the Indians pushed, pried, and pulled the *Duchess* into deep water. Steamboating had come to the Upper Columbia River.

During 1886 business wasn't extra buoyant, but next year volume increased. The stimulus was settlers lured West by the newly completed Canadian Pacific Railway and fears that Kootenay Indians were about to scalp the whites.

The uprising started with the murder of two prospectors and arrest of an Indian suspect. But Chief Isodore of the band involved didn't agree with the detective work. He paid the whites a visit, and with his braves holding cocked Winchesters as persuaders, soon had the prisoner released. He demanded also that the pair who arrested the brave, Harry Anderson and F. W. Aylmer, leave the area. They did.

In their place, however, arrived a detachment of 75 North West Mounted Police under Major Sam Steele. Their destination was the potential trouble region of Wild Horse Creek, some 180 miles south of Golden. Eventually they got there, but not without problems.

At Golden Major Steele hired the *Duchess* to transport his detachment the first 100 miles, freight .75 cents a hundred pounds with no guaranteed schedule. The latter clause indicated that Captain Armstrong didn't have total confidence in his vessel. Nor did the *Duchess* betray his judgment. She promptly capsized, taking with her officers' uniforms, horse feed, supplies and ammunition. Hoping for better luck, Major Steele hired the *Clive,* the only other vessel on the river. This decision contained an inevitable consequence since the *Clive* was an even worse tub than the *Duchess.*

She was the creation of "a scatterbrained young Canadian" named Jack Hayes. Her lines were not unlike a sack of potatoes, the only difference between bow and stern a paddlewheel on one end. But since her hull was originally a railway barge built of four-inch planks, her squarish design was understandable. She was sturdy enough, but this sturdiness was not all asset. As her owner admitted: "It made her sit kinder heavy in the water."

An upright boiler once part of a Manitoba steam plough and some odds and ends from a small tug became the power supply. Hayes didn't know how to assemble the assorted pieces but fate evidently admired his venturesome spirit. Along came a British sportsman-promoter-author named W. A. Baillie-Grohman. Not only did he have with him a mechanic who fitted the pieces together, but also a sawmill which provided some parts lacking in Hayes' assortment. Since Baillie-Grohman faced the formidable problem of transporting his sawmill—including a 5,000-pound boiler— some 100 miles upstream to the Columbia's headwaters, he also supplied the *Clive* with her first cargo.

On her maiden voyage, the home-made craft quickly demonstrated a disadvantage of sitting "kinder heavy in the water." The struggling steam plough engine was barely able to keep her from being washed downstream. Of the voyage, Baillie-Grohman wrote: "Nothing quite so odd as this piledriver, steam-plough, sawmill combination steamer has, I am sure, ever navigated water, and as we took twenty-three days to cover the hundred miles, our rate of progression can easily be calculated. . . . Since she had no cabins the only dry place was the sawmill boiler . . . towed on a sort of raft. I bagged it for my sleeping quarters, a sensible dog whom I found curled up in the firebox the first afternoon we were out giving me a lead in this bright idea."

To Baillie-Grohman, however, spartan living was no hardship. Although his mother was a cousin of the Duke of Wellington of Waterloo fame, he gravitated not to aristocracy but to the outdoors. He loved mountain climbing, hiking, shooting and similar sports. At 9 he shot his first deer; at 24 he wrote a very successful book *Tyrol and the Tyrolese*.

At 31 he had written several more books and made four hunting trips to the virtually uninhabited mountains of Western U.S. and Canada. On one of these journeys he saw the Kootenay Flats region of B.C., a 25-mile-long, 50,000-acre expanse of river-bottom land flanking the Kootenay River from the U.S. border to Kootenay Lake. Its potential was immense but at every freshet it flooded. Grohman, though, felt he could prevent the flooding. He would simply widen the outlet of Kootenay Lake, thus transforming the flats into a rich farming area. Then his hunting activities took him to the headwaters of both the Kootenay and Columbia Rivers. Here he formed a new plan—one that later proved disastrous to him and his backers.

The Columbia River is born at Columbia Lake on the western flank of the Rockies, while the Kootenay is born in the heart of the Rockies. But the Kootenay punches free of the mountains only a mile from Columbia Lake, with just a gravel flat between. Since the lake is 11 feet lower than the river, Grohman felt that the easiest way to prevent flooding at Kootenay Flats would be a ditch to divert the Kootenay into the Columbia.

He convinced the B.C. Government that his plan was practical and on December 10, 1883 signed a 10-year lease to 47,500 acres of prime land at Kootenay Flats. But before he dug a shovel into the gravel he met an obstacle. The Federal Government had final say on the diversion plan and on behalf of the Canadian Pacific Railway it opposed the diversion. The C.P.R., then building its trans-continental line, had located miles of track along the Columbia River. Diverting Kootenay water into the Columbia would raise the river level and mean relocating much of the new line.

The agreement was consequently re-negotiated. The final draft stipulated that instead of a ditch between Kootenay River and Columbia Lake, there would be a navigable canal with a 100- x 30-foot lock. Of more importance—and a disaster for Baillie-Grohman—flood waters of the Kootenay could not be diverted into the Columbia. As Grohman later admitted, at that point he should have dropped the project. But he didn't. Consequently, in 1886 he arrived in Golden with his sawmill to cut lumber for the lock and embarked on his memorable 23-day upstream journey on the *Clive*.

When the *Clive* finally arrived back at Golden after delivering the sawmill she was hired by Major Steele, still annoyed about his watery experience with the *Duchess*. He was even more annoyed when Hayes, his opposition under water, raised rates from .75 cents a hundred to $1. Unfor-

The first Duchess, upper right, was no floating palace. The Marion, center, wasn't much better. She offered standing room only. Opposite is Golden in 1883.

tunately, inflated cargo rates were no guarantee of delivery. To Major Steele's astonishment the *Clive* also sank. As she settled to the bottom her cargo of yellow oats and scarlet tunics mixed to make a "colorful assortment as they drifted along the surface of the water."

By the time the exasperated Major Steele had his oats, ammunition, and uniforms replaced, the Indian scare had subsided. Nevertheless the policemen, this time on horseback, headed up the Columbia then down the Kootenay Valley. At a place called Galbraith's Ferry they built barracks and other buildings. But this large force proved unnecessary and a year later they left. To commemorate them the community was renamed Fort Steele in honor of Major Steele. Possibly of greater satisfaction to the police commander was the knowledge that brief as his stay was, he outlasted both the *Clive* and the *Duchess*.

After their wet adventure with the Mounted Police they were raised, but the *Clive's* career thereupon ended. The *Duchess* sailed for the rest of the 1887 season then her

ancient machinery was installed in a new vessel. This time Captain Armstrong had access to both a sawmill and money. He hired Alexander Watson, one of the province's master craftsmen, to build his new vessel. The result was a sparkling *Duchess* with such luxuries as individual cabins and a dining saloon.

Armstrong also built a smaller sternwheeler, the *Marion*, although she didn't ply the Upper Columbia for long. In 1889 in a display of sternwheeler adaptability she was hoisted aboard two flatcars and shipped to Revelstoke. Replacing her was the *Pert*, a sidewheeler converted from a 50-foot bateau originally built by prospector Fred Wells. He later discovered gold in the Cariboo and is commemorated by the community of Wells.

In 1892 another sternwheeler, the *Hyak*, joined the growing fleet. In commenting on the launching, one paper noted that: "The steamboats and outfit owned by the company are valued at $150,000." The company referred to was the Upper Columbia River Navigation and Tramway Company. It was

The second Duchess, above, was a superior vessel to the original homespun version. In 1887 two roving English authors, Lees and Clutterbuck, travelled on the first Duchess. Of the trip, they wrote: "... we lunched on the Duchess with the captain, Mr. Armstrong. ... His craft presented a somewhat decrepit appearance, as about a fortnight before our arrival she had been wrecked in the Columbia with a full cargo and some passengers. They had managed to fish her up again out of about fourteen feet of water, and she was now in steaming order ...."

The Duchess started an informal style of postal service, for as Lees and Clutterbuck noted: "... a ranchman came down and mentioned that he had a letter to send in the morning by the return boat, and would just stick it out over the river on a long pole to be caught as she flew past. ..." The practice became so popular that Captain Armstrong's company finally decided to charge for handling mail. They printed their own stamps and sold them at 5 cents each. Everyone was happy until Federal postal officials learned of the arrangement and quickly squelched it.

formed by Captain Armstrong to provide a continuous service from Golden some 180 miles to Fort Steele. As part of the system the Company built two tramways: a two-mile section between the C.P.R. station and sternwheel landing at Golden, and a five-mile section to parallel a shallow, rapid-ripped section of Columbia River between Adela and Columbia Lakes.

The region had now changed remarkably from the day in 1882 when Baillie-Grohman arrived and found fewer than 20 white settlers in the entire Kootenay. There were new communities and roads, thousands of mining claims staked, farms established, and between 1890-93 alone, 11 railways incorporated. The most important was the Crow's Nest and Kootenay Lake Railway intended to link Kootenay Lake to eastern Canada via Fort Steele and Crow's Nest Pass. Its charter lapsed but in 1894 the project was revised as the B.C. Southern. In 1896 construction started.

Meanwhile to the south the Great Northern Railway had been completed across the Western States to Seattle. It reach-ed the Kootenay River at Jennings, Montana, some 150 miles downstream from Fort Steele. Since this section of river was navigable, ore from Kootenay mines now could be profitably shipped to smelters in Montana and Washington. This development further stimulated mining activity. New ore bodies discovered included one at Mark Creek that ultimately proved the world's largest deposit of silver-lead-zinc and created the city of Kimberley. It also resulted in several sternwheelers appearing on the Upper Kootenay

First was the *Annerly*. She arrived at Fort Steele on her maiden voyage from Jennings in May 1893. A modest craft, she carried 50 tons of freight and what passengers could squeeze aboard. Since she had neither galley nor cabins, men slept on the deck. Women had more elaborate accommodation—a mattress in a curtained-off corner. They also ate with the captain but men provided their own facilities. One woman passenger recorded that a group of prospectors "cooked their meals over a sheet of tin on a coal stove in the middle of the boat."

The Annerly, above, had accommodation almost as spartan as that on the Marion, a sternwheeler without even a cabin. In 1888 Mrs. A. St. Maur, later Duchess of Somerset, travelled on the Marion and wrote: "There was a board roof . . . with canvas hanging at the sides, which afforded some shelter against the rain, which came down in torrents. The passengers sat shivering round the funnel of the steamer. . . ." Later at the Windermere Hotel Mrs. St. Maur experienced another aspect of life in frontier B.C. Women were scarce and when a group of men got together they frequently held a "Bull's Ball." She wrote: "After we had gone to bed, there was too much noise to allow us to sleep and the drunken orgie ended in what they called a Bull's Ball. A fiddler arrived, about thirty men danced together, and the shuffling of feet and the talking and the laughing, and the reek of bad tobacco, disturbed us until an early hour the next morning."

To counter this modest competition, Captain Armstrong started constructing a new sternwheeler to provide an "all-Canadian route" from the C.P.R. at Golden to Fort Steele. She was the *Gwendoline*, a vessel destined to have some unusual experiences, including rolling off a freight train.

She was launched at Hansen's Landing 12 miles above Fort Steele, then sailed to Golden for fitting out. By now Baillie-Grohman had completed his lock at a cost of $100,000, but it contributed nothing to his reclamation project and the entire scheme was abandoned. The *Gwendoline* became the first vessel to use the lock and canal, although not without problems. Before she could squeeze through the lock had to be partly dismantled and the vessel shoved and pulled through on rollers.

She was completed during the winter and on May 22, 1894 sailed again for the Upper Kootenay. She arrived at Fort Steele six days later, adding another first to her record. She became the only vessel to make a return trip through Grohman's Canal.

Another skipper who built a sternwheeler at Hansen's Landing was Captain Tom Flowers. In 1894 his *Fool Hen* splashed into the Kootenay River. She was a unique vessel. "He must have built it by the dark of the moon. . ." wrote Bill Doak in Mrs. D. W. Johnson's book *The Story of the Tobacco Plains Country*. ". . . he installed machinery which he had procured . . . in exchange for fifteen cayuses. Her machinery was too large for the hull, leaving no room for freight, but it surely could travel. The wheel was filled on the paddles by tops from packing cases, and furnished a rather amusing advertisement for . . . Libby merchants. When the wheel began business the spectator would see John P. Wall, Neff and Plummer, and Allan B. Johnston following each other like a merry-go-round."

Flowers quickly dismantled the *Fool Hen* and placed her machinery in another hull which he named *Libby*. This time, by contrast, the hull was too big for the machinery. After a couple of trips she was dismantled. The failures didn't unduly bother Tom Flowers. As one paper observed: "Captain Tom is a rustler and is bound to get there."

The failure of his creations was unfortunate for Captain Tom since freight was abundant. From the rich North Star mine on Mark Creek a 21-mile road connected to the Kootenay River. Over it horse-drawn wagons transported thousands of tons of ore to North Star Landing for shipment downstream. Stimulated by the mining bonanza, Fort Steele thrived. Seven saloons hummed day and night, while mining speculators and real estate promoters prospered. The community even had a newspaper, the *Fort Steele Prospector*. For 1896 its editor predicted that mineral production would probably be $3 million, even $5 million, population would continue to grow and a smelter might be a possibility.

On March 14 the paper announced the appearance of a new firm, International Transportation Company. Its owners included Captain Armstrong, Jim Wardner, and J. D. Miller, a veteran U.S. sternwheel skipper. The company planned to operate sternwheelers on the entire 300-mile waterway from Jennings to Golden. For this service the *Gwendoline* would be rebuilt and a new sternwheeler added.

The latter vessel was the *Ruth*, launched April 23, 1896. The finest sternwheeler yet to appear, she could carry 100 tons of freight and for her passengers offered a dining saloon, smoking room, and individual staterooms. Commanded by Captain J. D. Miller she arrived at Fort Steele on May 27 "after making a remarkably quick trip, coming up in two days."

Superintendent Samuel B. Steele, commander of the 75 N.W.M.P. who arrived at Galbraith's Ferry August 1, 1887. In 30 years of service, Steele became a legend. During the Klondike rush he was in charge of police posts on both White and Chilkoot Passes, and in 1898-99 all of B.C.-Yukon. He served in both the Boer War and the First World War.

W. A. Baillie-Grohman in his study in Austria. For him, the Kootenay venture was a disaster. He worked 9 years on his reclamation project, crossed the Atlantic over 30 times, and reclaimed not an acre. The reclamation scheme lost a fortune, but despite this discouraging experience Grohman still referred to British Columbia as a "land of great beauty and promising future."

Another newcomer was the *Rustler*, but she piled up in Jennings Canyon before she was six weeks old. The Canyon, a boulder-strewn, 70-foot-wide constriction with an elbow bend, was extremely treacherous. "The water follows the

Fort Steele at its peak development and the sternwheeler Ruth at low water in the Kootenay. Like most frontier communities, Fort Steele was virtually isolated in winter and the first sternwheeler in spring resulted in a celebration. On May 1, 1897 the Fort Steele Prospector noted: "Tuesday was a day of excitement and . . . every inhabitant who could was either on the bluff overlooking the river or at the bridge to welcome the Gwendoline, the first steamer of the season. Gaily she came up the river decked with flags fluttering in the bright sunshine, and as she neared town she was fittingly received by a voluntary salute of 21 guns. She had a goodly list of passengers and a full cargo of merchandise." The Gwendoline also brought the first church bell to Fort Steele, its "silver tone announcing its presence."

left bank," wrote Captain Armstrong, "but is so piled up against it that a large vessel cannot follow it, her own gravity making her slide off to the right and so onto the rocks.

"Our way to negotiate the place was to stop the engines before we got to the elbow, and start backing as soon as we were abreast of it. That would throw the stern into the eddy under the point, her bow would sweep away from the right bank and by giving 'full speed ahead' while still heading for the rocks, the current would take us past them into smooth water." Since the current swept a sternwheeler from the elbow to the rocks in 11 seconds, skippers were never more than a wrong move from disaster. Of six sternwheelers which challenged the Canyon, five were to be badly battered or completely wrecked.

On her fatal voyage the *Rustler* struck a rock and stove in her hull beneath the boiler. Luckily, the *Annerly* had preceded her through and Captain Sandborn's wife noticed that the *Rustler* was in grave trouble. Captain Sandborn swung back into the Canyon and rescued her 19 passengers and crew. A few minutes later the *Rustler* washed off the rock, rolled over, threw out her boiler and 60 tons of cargo and floated downstream a tangle of wreckage.

Next year on May 7 the Canyon smashed both the *Ruth* and the *Gwendoline*. The *Ruth*, on her second trip of the season, rammed a rock in the channel and partly climbed up it. Passengers scrambled for its comparative safety but there wasn't room for everyone. Fortunately, purser Bill Doak got a boat free and ferried everyone safely ashore.

Less than an hour later the *Gwendoline* steamed into the Canyon, Captain Armstrong unaware that the *Ruth* blocked the main channel. "Her nose was on one of the rocks and her wheel near the right bank." he later recalled. "There was nothing for it but go full speed ahead and try to make the channel to the left of the rocks. . . . she didn't make it quite, . . . she struck amidships . . . with a great portion of her starboard side torn away. What with the crashing of timber, hissing of broken steam pipes, roar of the water, the din was tremendous."

She still floated, although only the strong current kept her from sliding off the rock and sinking. Captain Armstrong eased the strain by dumping her cargo. Then two days later a drop in the river enabled the crew to build a temporary bulkhead and float the battered vessel to a nearby beach. Here she was lashed to a barge and taken to Jennings for repairs.

Captain Miller felt that bad judgment by Captain Sandborn caused the loss, especially since the Company had removed the worst rocks from Jennings Canyon only a few months previously. Captain Sandborn blamed a log in the *Ruth's* rudder for his trouble. Captain Miller, however, wasn't impressed with the explanation. Equally annoying to him was that after the *Ruth* blocked the channel, Captain Sandborn didn't attempt to flag the *Gwendoline*, even though Mrs. Sandborn had twice suggested he do so.

The mishap was a severe blow to the Company because they lost not only the vessels but also some $40,000 in freight revenue. By June, however, prospects were more cheerful. The *Gwendoline* was again in service and a new vessel ready. She was the *North Star*. When she arrived at Fort Steele on her maiden voyage the local paper reported her ". . . a beautiful specimen of swift water craft. . . the largest boat ever built, or run on the Kootenay. . . ."

Under command of Captain Miller she completed 21 profitable trips before September low water halted navigation. Downstream she hauled jute sacks of ore, 16 to the ton, 100 tons a trip. Upstream she brought food and liquor, clothing and building supplies, miners, speculators and others attracted by the booming Fort Steele district.

By now real estate firms promoted the district with full page newspaper advertisements. "KOOTENAY'S CAPITAL" headlined one. Then it stated that Fort Steele had a population of 1,500 and within three months could expect 5,000. Businesses included a bank, eight hotels, five large general stores, two sawmills plus a selection of saloons, "all in active operation."

The editor of the *Fort Steele Prospector*, A. B. Guthrie, was equally optimistic. "Fort Steele," he wrote, "is the natural center to which must flow all the trade from the vast . . . mineral country to the east and north. This trade is certain of itself to be sufficient to support a city of 10,000. . . ."

In a previous issue he commented on the B.C. Southern Railway that was under construction between Lethbridge and Kootenay Lake. ". . . we do not claim that the crossing (of the Kootenay River) will be made at Fort Steele, but we do claim there is every probability—we might also say it is certainty—that the present and future capital of the district, to wit, Fort Steele, will be an important station on the main line of the new railway. There is no insurmountable obstacle in the way." Unfortunately for the community, there was an insurmountable obstacle in the way. Because of it Fort Steele wasn't to be an important station on the railway. It wasn't, in fact, even to be on the railway.

But as 1896 closed, the future looked as cheerful as a full moon over the spires of the nearby Rockies. Business boomed, new railways were incorporated—10 during 1897-98 alone—and in November another sternwheeler was launched at Jennings. She was the $20,000 J. D. Farrell, largest and most comfortable to sail the Upper Kootenay.

She arrived at Fort Steele on her maiden voyage on April 28, 1898, welcomed by the local band and "a salute of dynamite sticks." Because of low water, her first trip took 12 days instead of the expected 24 hours. She arrived with her paddlewheel worn thin from "being aground on every bar from Jennings to Fort Steele." On one bar below Elk River she stranded five days. The only casualty was her own bar, which ran dry. This dismaying development was a potential disaster for the dry-throated miners, but new supplies were hurried overland by horseback and a crisis averted.

A few days after the J. D. Farrell left Jennings, Captain J. D. Miller started upstream with the North Star, her cargo $30,000 worth of liquor and goods for Forte Steele Mercantile Company. But near the rocks that wrecked the Rustler she had a hole knocked in her hull large enough "to put a wagon box through." Using skill gained from commanding over 30 vessels during a lifetime on turbulent rivers, Captain Miller beached her, hauled her onto a makeshift ways, and a week later was again underway.

The J. D. Farrell was less fortunate. On her seventh trip she was buffeted by hurricane winds in the Canyon. Blown out of control, she veered into the rocks and ripped a ragged chunk from her side. She was run ashore where she settled with only bow and capstan above water. Later she was salvaged but by then sternwheelers were no longer practical on Upper Kootenay.

On October 5 the last spike was driven in the B.C. Southern Railway. The profitable cargoes of ore, liquor, and merchandise which had sustained the sternwheelers now went by rail. The three vessels on the river—Gwendoline, North Star, and J. D. Farrell—were tied up, soon to

At upper left the Isabella McCormick churns into Lake Windermere and, opposite, the J. D. Farrell in winter quarters at Jennings, Montana. When the J. D. Farrell arrived at Fort Steele on her maiden voyage April 28, 1898 the Fort Steele Prospector described her as: ". . . a very shapely boat, fitted with elegant staterooms, bath rooms, dining room, etc. illuminated with electric lights, (and) carries a powerful searchlight which enables her to travel as safely by night as by day. The arrival of the steamer at the wharf here was signalized by a salute of dynamite sticks. The Fort Steele brass band was on hand. . . . Almost the entire town turned out to witness the arrival. . . ."

live only in the pages of history. Joining them was Fort Steele.

The problem, recalls old-timer J. Eric Sowerby, was that "a small group of the city fathers and property owners figured that the C.P.R. (owners of the B.C. Southern) would pay handsomely for space in Fort Steele. However, they sharpened their pencils too much so the railway company decided to by-pass the community rather than pay the prices asked for the property."

The line crossed Kootenay River at Wardner, some 18 miles south of Fort Steele, effectively strangling the pioneer settlement. Replacing it as the commercial center for the district was a new community called Cranbrook. It was laid out on Colonel Hyde Baker's ranch in the spring of 1897 and the first building, the Cranbrook Hotel, opened December 23. On July 27, 1898, tracks reached the area and businessmen began moving from Fort Steele.

Meanwhile, Captain Armstrong and other steamboatmen had been attracted north by the Klondike stampede. Two years later when the goldrush excitement waned, the Captain returned. He learned that in his absence the *Gwendoline* had ended her career in a way both original and unusual.

The episode began when Captain Miller decided to take her to Kootenay Lake for use on the Lardeau River. Since part of the Kootenay River below Libby is unnavigable, in June 1899 she was loaded aboard three flat cars and headed to Canada. The trip was dramatically short. Three miles below Kootenay Falls station the tracks paralleled a rock face. In an attempt to squeeze by, the *Gwendoline* was shifted to one side of the flat cars, overbalanced, and plummeted 50 feet into the Canyon. As the *Libby News* reported: "She turned over in the fall and lit on her smokestack and is there now, not worth a bad 50-cent piece, with her bottom up and flat as a pancake." In addition to losing the vessel, Captain Miller had to pay $500 freight charges.

In 1901 the *J. D. Farrell* ended her Kootenay days. She was purchased for $6,000 by railway contractors A. Guthrie and Company, who also chartered the *North Star*. During the summer the pair helped build a branch line of the Great Northern Railway from Rexford, Montana via Fernie to the Crows Nest coalfield. By autumn their work ended and the *J. D. Farrell* was later dismantled and shipped to Lake Pend d'Orielle. The *North Star* was the last to go. On October 18 Captain Miller sold his interest in her to the Upper Columbia Navigation Company and next spring Captain Armstrong sailed her north to Golden. It was a remarkable voyage even for vessels that habitually made the impossible routine.

Among obstacles the 132-foot-long vessel faced was the 100-foot-long lock in Baillie-Grohman's canal. In addition, she was nine inches wider than the lock, unable to pass under a bridge spanning Columbia River, and too deep draft for the shallow river. Nevertheless on June 4, 1902 Captain Armstrong cast off from Fort Steele and headed the *North Star* upstream. She was the last sternwheeler to leave the faltering community.

"NORTH STAR IS COMING" said an optimistic headline in the *Wilmer Outcrop* on June 12. To sweating crewmen the headline was premature; at the time a garden slug could have outpaced them. Squeezing the vessel through the Canal took two weeks, but since many considered the task impossible, such progress was speedy.

The problem of passing the 130-foot-long vessel through

the 100-foot lock Captain Armstrong solved by burning out the lock gates and building temporary ones of ore sacks filled with sand. The width problem was easier—he simply trimmed her guard rails. When all was ready dynamite was tamped into the sandbag lock and fuse lit. Amidst the resulting eruption of sand, sacking, mud and water the *North Star* surged into the Columbia watershed, her "deep bass whistle echoing . . . and re-echoing from peak to peak of the Rocky and Selkirk Mountains."

She inched down the sluffed-in Canal to Columbia Lake then into the Columbia River, her hull dragging bottom, her superstructure in the brush. At one point a tree crashed into her, narrowly missing the Captain's young daughter, Ruth. There was a delay at the road crossing while the bridge was hoisted with the vessel's capstan, placed on a temporary support, then returned after she passed beneath. She reached Golden on July 2, her crew wondering whether they had sailed or pushed her downstream.

In honor of the voyage Wilmer citizens held a banquet

The Ptarmigan with sacks of ore on her blunt foredeck. Since many mines were high in the mountains and inaccessible by road, a common method of moving ore was by "rawhiding." About a ton of ore was laced into a cowhide, several hides chained together, then a horse hauled them down the snow-covered mountain trails.

on July 19, guests including prominent citizens from Windermere, Athalmer, Fort Steele, Golden and other communities. Among courses were salmon, roast chicken, beef, mutton, plum pudding, ice-cream, strawberries plus a wine list that "contained a plenteous variety." The latter was fortunate since speeches were as prevalent as June mosquitoes. Toasts included one to His Majesty, the U.S. president, the provincial legislature, mineral industry, the press, ladies, legal profession, and virtually anyone else who came to mind.

In expressing his thanks Captain Armstrong pointed out that greatest credit was due to Mr. Woods, the ship's carpenter, and Mr. Davis, the engineer. He said that there had been times when "he was discouraged and at the point of giving up, but these men never wavered."

After her unduplicated voyage the *North Star* made several trips on the Columbia but proved too big for the river. Next year another problem developed. Since she was built in Jennings she was classed as American, thus subject to

duty when she entered Canada. Captain Armstrong ignored this red tape so Canadian Customs seized her, a development which bothered Captain Armstrong not a bit. He simply left her tied up at Golden and over the years "borrowed" pieces for inclusion in his other vessels.

During the years that Captain Armstrong had been sailing on the Upper Kootenay River little change had occurred on the Upper Columbia. In 1899 Captain H. E. Forster shipped his small *Selkirk* via C.P.R. from the Thompson River but she wasn't used commercially. Another newcomer, Captain Alexander Blakely, bought the sidewheeler *Pert* and eventually rebuilt her into a propeller-driven vehicle.

The *Duchess*, meanwhile, became involved in the "affair of the stolen church." The episode began in 1899 when the C.P.R. decided to move its divisional point from Donald, 16 miles downstream from Golden, to Revelstoke. Buildings and people moved west, with the notable exception of pioneer merchant Rufus Kimpton. He headed for Lake Windermere, some 100 miles up the Columbia River from

The Selkirk *on the Upper Columbia River and St. Peter's Church at Windermere. Rufus Kimpton, the man who decided to "borrow" the church, passed away in Windermere on July 2, 1934 at the age of 74. In later years there was a sequel to the incident which has made St. Peter's Church a legend.*

In October 1967 some Windermere residents decided to reunite their famous church and its 600-pound bell. In a manner that would have pleased Rufus, they helped themselves to the bell from the church at Golden and left their own. However, the silver-toned bell didn't peal very long from St. Peter's. The bishop decided that such pilfering, however well motivated, wasn't quite right and the bell is now back in Golden, closing the saga of the stolen church.

Golden. His wife, however, wasn't too happy in her new home.

In Donald she and her husband had helped build St. Peter's Anglican Church and she now missed the church and church work. Rufus, a forthright man, decided to solve her problem. He would bring the church to her. There was, though, one possible obstacle—it had already been promised to Revelstoke. But Rufus reasoned that no-one had denied him permission to take the Church, and promptly dismantled the building and shipped it to Golden. Here it was loaded onto a barge, its 600-pound bell displayed prominantly on top. But when the *Duchess* was about to start upstream with her pilfered cargo, the bell was gone. Rufus immediately suspected a conspiracy. Worse, he felt that Golden's magistrate, Griff Griffith, was involved and said so.

The result appears in the book *Golden Memories*, published by the Golden Historical Committee:

"Some son-of-a-gun stole the bell," Rufus complained.

The magistrate looked at him straightfaced. "Go on home. Some son-of-a-gun stole the whole church."

"Keep the danged bell," retorted Rufus. "It's so heavy it shakes the Church to pieces anyway."

Soon after the bell-less church was in its new location overlooking Windermere Lake. Then letters travelled downstream to Golden demanding return of the stolen bell. Others came upstream from Revelstoke demanding return of the entire church. Eventually the incident faded into memory, but not until 1905 did miffed church officials relent and consecrate the church.

By then the *Duchess* had been retired and her venerable power plant—now over 60 years old—installed in a new sternwheeler, the *Ptarmigan*.

She was the last vessel built for the Upper Columbia Navigation and Tramway Company. Shortly afterward the Columbia River Lumber Company bought the pioneer firm. The sale severed a link with early pioneer days, as did an announcement by the C.P.R. that it intended to build a railway from Golden via the Upper Columbia and Koot-

The North Star on her last voyage on the Kootenay River before Captain Armstrong brought her north to the Columbia. In 1906 Captain N. Cantlie, an eccentric Scot, challenged Captain Armstrong, who then commanded the Ptarmigan, to a race. Cantlie owned a gas launch, the Gian, drank champagne for breakfast and kept a piper in full Highland regalia as a personal attendant. The August 25, 1906 issue of the Golden Star carried a headline THE GREAT BOAT RACE. The story read, in part: "The Gian passed the Ptarmigan . . . with colours flying and full speed ahead, sailing gracefully by with her piper at the stern playing Bonnie Dundee. Captain Armstrong . . . his Irish blood circulating as it never had before, took to the middle of the stream and gave chase. He was after that piper and meant to have him."

The Ptarmigan gradually gained, the piper keeping up an incessant drone to the annoyance of Captain Armstrong, "whose mad kept getting madder all the time." Finally the Ptarmigan caught the Gian and "two or three able-bodied seamen grabbed that piper who by this time was playing The Cock of the North . . . and lifted him bodily from the stern of the launch and placed him safely on the deck of the steamer, the piper in the meantime never losing a single note. . . ."

To Captain Armstrong's satisfaction, the Ptarmigan won.

enay Rivers to its B.C. Southern line at Wardner. Completion of the line would mean the end of sternwheel days on the Upper Columbia, although construction proved a long-term project. Surveys started in 1904 but not until 1915 was the last spike driven.

During construction of the line, sternwheel activity continued. In 1908 the *Ptarmigan* was replaced with the *Isabella McCormick*, later renamed *Isabell*. She wasn't a success, even though she was the fastest vessel to appear on the river. In 1910 she was tied up at Athalmer at the outlet of Lake Windermere and converted into a floating hotel, her machinery transferred to a new sternwheeler, the *Klahowya*.

For her, Captain Armstrong used a unique method of construction. Her framework was built in New Westminster, then shipped to Golden where the Captain had built a ways on the ice of the Columbia River. To launch her he simply cut the ice and let her settle into the water. With the *Klahowya* Captain Armstrong hoped to capitalize on the growing tourist traffic. Designed to accommodate 100 passengers, she was "fitted up very luxuriously . . . ."

In 1911 the *Klahowya* was joined by the *Nowitka*, a sternwheeler that, in the words of Captain Armstrong, "would make a splendid nucleus of a museum of early steamboating". Her boiler was from a sawmill; her engines those used in the Montreal ferry in 1840, the original *Duchess* in 1886, the second *Duchess*, and the *Ptarmigan*; her pilothouse and capstan came from the *North Star*, as did the helm which had originally been part of the *City of Salem* on the Willamette River; while among her cutlery were C.P.R. souvenir spoons plus a variety of other odds and ends. Despite her hybrid origin, she was to close commercial sternwheel service on the Upper Columbia.

She wasn't, however, the last sternwheeler constructed. That distinction went to the *F. P. Armstrong*. She was built in 1913 for Burns and Jordon, railway contractors for the Kootenay Central Railway. She operated only a year, then completion of the railway and World War 1 virtually ended Upper Columbia River sternwheel days.

Captain John Blakely, far left, was the last of the Upper Columbia sternwheel captains. He served his apprenticeship under his father, Captain A. Blakely, and Captain Armstrong. During the First World War he was one of six survivors when his vessel was blown up in the English Channel. After the War he returned to East Kootenay, learned to fly and in 1929 owned the first aeroplane in the region. He made his last sternwheel voyage in 1960. Then 71, he commanded the Keno down the Yukon River from Whitehorse to Dawson City.

At right the Klahowya churns the Columbia River near Golden in 1912. The F.P. Armstrong, above, was named after the pioneer captain, shown at left on the first Duchess in 1887. During the First World War Captain Armstrong served with distinction on the Tigris and Nile Rivers, where he was superintendent of all military vessels. On his return to the Kootenays he was employed by the Dominion Government but was seriously injured in Nelson. He died in Vancouver General Hospital January 26, 1923. Of him an old-timer wrote: "With Armstrong those who could pay were expected and those who couldn't were never left stranded."

In May, 1920, Captain F. P. Armstrong made the last trip upstream in the *Nowitka*. Of the trip he wrote: "Thirty-four years almost to a day, after the first steamer sailed up the Columbia River from Golden, another left the same place to drive piles for a bridge at Brisco, half way to Windermere, thus closing navigation for good and all."

But the beat of paddlewheel on the Upper Columbia had not yet entirely stilled. In 1948 Captain John Blakely built a small sternwheeler for his own use. Because of the low bridges at Brisco she was little more than a floating box, but she did have two staterooms, a galley, and a large saloon. In an article in *BC Outdoors* magazine Louise McFadden wrote: "The boat was launched by Mrs. Blakely and christened the *Radium Queen* and with Captain Blakely in the wheelhouse she churned out into the eddying currents of the river on her maiden voyage. As she passed the bends familiar to so many vanished boats—the *Duchess, Marion, Clive, Gwendoline, North Star* and many others, it was as if she were surrounded by a fleet of old friends. Captain

Blakely knew them all, at first or second hand, their personality, and their history.

"Captain Blakely would point out, between Radium and Invermere, the remains of the second *Duchess;* near Fairmont, the skeleton of the *F. P. Armstrong* where she had been abandoned on completion of the Kootenay Central Railway; and by the pilings of the old sawmill wharf at Golden, the bones of the *Nowitka,* enfolding the ancient engines which once served the *Duchess.*

"Each time he made the trip there remained of the old days even less to see. The years passed. Increasingly the people he met were surprised to hear that commercial sternwheelers had ever operated on the river. Soon, it seemed, there would be no one to remember the steamers and the men with their individuality and enterprise, and there would be nothing left of the riverboats."

Soon these predictions came true. Captain Blakely died in 1963. With him went the last strong link with the East Kootenay days of "Steamboat 'Round the Bend."

114

NASOOKIN.

CHAPTER NINE

Arrow and Kootenay Lakes

"Upon the draining of a few bottles of Hudson Bay (rum) by the people of the steamer . . . the vessel started up the river on her trial trip. She performed the trip with skill and power, turning back at the upper end of the Lower Columbia Arrow Lake, with the thermometer at 28 degrees below zero. If it had not been for the ice forming in the river . . . the Rapids of the Dead, 260 miles above Colville, would have been reached. . . ."

It was December 1865 and the sternwheeler was the *Forty-Nine,* launched just below the B.C.-Washington border on November 18th "By the light of some candles, and fitful glimpses of the polar star. . . ." A flourishing gold rush was on to a region of the Columbia River known as the "Big Bend," and with the *Forty-Nine* Captain Leonard White planned to supply the food-short miners who had rushed to the region. The frozen Arrow Lake thwarted his plans and not until April could he again sail north.

This time the *Forty-Nine* reached La Porte near the foot of Death Rapids, pioneering a 260-mile section of the Columbia River in B.C. Captain White unloaded his impatient passengers and headed down the Columbia for more. But the miners quickly discovered that the gold in the gravel didn't match the gold in the rumors. On his third trip upstream Captain White carried 3 paying passengers. Nevertheless he ran the vessel until 1869 when his health failed and he retired.

First mate A. F. Pingston took over but in October the *Forty-Nine* sliced open her hull and was beached below Downie Creek. She was patched and taken to Colville, Washington, although on June 26, 1870, the *Victoria Colonist* noted that she "Won't resume trips for a long time." After that she was used only spasmodically; then, like the gold rush she was built to serve, she faded quietly into history.

Not until 1884 did the region again echo the blast of a steam whistle. The new arrival was the *Midge,* brought in by W. A. Baillie-Grohman to help in his land reclamation project. She wasn't a sternwheeler, but she was the first

The Nasookin was the largest sternwheeler to ply B.C. waters. She was the pride of Nelson, always met by a welcoming crowd when she landed at the city wharf.

115

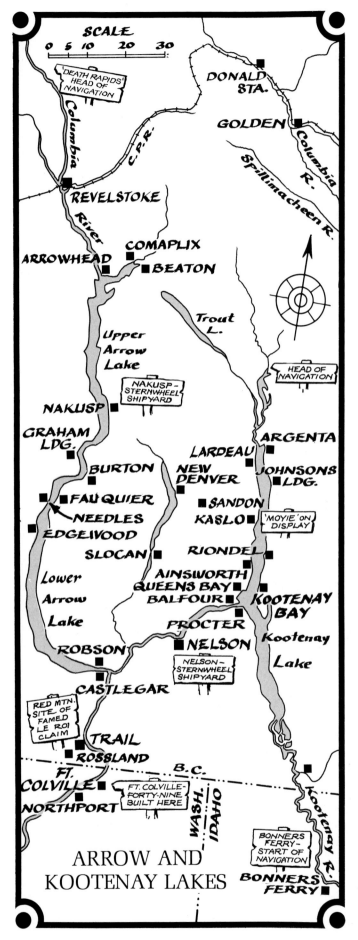

SCALE
0 5 10 20 30

"DEATH RAPIDS" HEAD OF NAVIGATION

DONALD STA.

GOLDEN

C.P.R.

Columbia River

Spillimacheen R.

Columbia R.

REVELSTOKE

COMAPLIX

ARROWHEAD

BEATON

Trout L.

Upper Arrow Lake

HEAD OF NAVIGATION

NAKUSP STERNWHEEL SHIPYARD

NAKUSP

GRAHAM LDG.

ARGENTA

LARDEAU

NEW DENVER

JOHNSONS LDG.

BURTON

FAUQUIER

SANDON

KASLO

"MOYIE" ON DISPLAY

NEEDLES

EDGEWOOD

SLOCAN

RIONDEL

AINSWORTH

Lower Arrow Lake

QUEENS BAY

BALFOUR

KOOTENAY BAY

PROCTER

Kootenay

ROBSON

NELSON

NELSON STERNWHEEL SHIPYARD

Kootenay Lake

CASTLEGAR

RED MTN. SITE OF FAMED LE ROI CLAIM

TRAIL

ROSSLAND

FT. COLVILLE

B.C.

FT. COLVILLE FORTY-NINE BUILT HERE

NORTHPORT

WASH. IDAHO

Kootenay R.

BONNERS FERRY START OF NAVIGATION

ARROW AND KOOTENAY LAKES

BONNERS FERRY

steam vessel to ply Kootenay Lake. Nor was she very big, which was just as well for she was carried by "a large force of Kootenay Indians and some 10 or 12 white men" over 39 miles of trail from the nearest railway, Sandpoint, Idaho, to Bonners Ferry on the Kootenay River.

Among local Indians the *Midge* caused considerable excitement. They enjoyed having their canoes towed, but their supreme satisfaction was tooting her whistle. Baillie-Grohman capitalized on these traits by exchanging tows and toots for piles of cordwood. "This was an economical way of solving a difficulty which besets most pioneer steamers," he noted with satisfaction.

The next year another sternwheeler appeared on the Columbia. She was the *Kootenai,* launched on April 25 at Little Dalles in Washington by Henderson and McCartney, railway contractors for the C.P.R. Under command of Captain A. L. Pingstone the 140-foot vessel embarked on her maiden voyage in May, hauling supplies and construction equipment over the route pioneered by the *Forty-Nine.* The *Kootenai* operated successfully all summer but with completion of the railway that November was tied up at Little Dalles.

Once again there was a lapse. Then in July 1888 a unique sternwheeler appeared on the Columbia River at Revelstoke. She was the *Despatch,* a small vessel with two hulls, the only catamaran sternwheeler to appear in B.C. Each hull was just over 54 feet long with the paddlewheel between.

She left Revelstoke on her maiden voyage August 8, bound for Sproat's Landing at the junction of the Columbia-Kootenay Rivers. She completed the round trip in 4 days with her owners, J. F. Hume, W. Cowan and Captain R. Sanderson, "satisfied that the steamer will work satisfactorily."

But, recalled John F. Hume, son of one of the original owners, she didn't live up to her promise. "For the first trips she ran with only one engine since Dad and his partners didn't have enough money to pay the freight on both engines and the freighter wouldn't release them without payment. She was a very cranky boat, especially in rough water since the effect was like having two canoes lashed side by side. Then she didn't have enough room for both wood and cargo. To make time she had to have lots of wood and little cargo. If the freight load was heavy she had to stop frequently to wood up. It was the failure of the boat, rather than the success, that caused Dad and his partners to expand."

This expansion brought into the original partnership three men long associated with pioneer transportation: Captain J. Irving from the Lower Fraser River, J. A. Mara from Kamloops and F. S. Barnard, whose father founded the B.C. Express Company of Cariboo gold rush fame. They launched a $100,000 firm, the Columbia and Kootenay Steam Navigation Company, or C.K.S.N. as it soon was called. They hired Captain James Troup, a prominent steamboatman from Oregon, as superintendent and in December confidently laid the keel of a $38,000 sternwheeler to replace the *Despatch.*

One of the reasons for their confidence was massive outcroppings of rich lead-silver-zinc and gold ore being developed throughout the Kootenay-Arrow region. And this confidence would prove well-founded. From less than $74,000 in 1890, mineral output soared to $781,000 within 4 years and to $6.5 million in 8. With this stimulus entire new communities appeared, including Rossland and Trail in 1890,

Slocan and Kaslo in 1891, Nakusp and Kimberley in 1892, Moyie in 1898 and Lardeau in 1902. In addition, railway rivalry and railway construction reached the stage where it was called "comic."

Main rivals were the C.P.R., the Spokane Falls and Northern, the Great Northern and their various subsidiaries. Lines built included the Nelson and Fort Sheppard which connected Nelson to the U.S. border; the Columbia and Kootenay which followed Kootenay River from Nelson to Sproat's Landing; a 27-mile C.P.R. spur line from Revelstoke to Arrowhead; the Nakusp and Slocan from Nakusp to Sandon; the Kaslo and Slocan from Kaslo to Sandon; the Red Mountain between Rossland and Northport; the Columbia and Western from Trail to Rossland; the B.C. Southern from Alberta through Fernie and Cranbrook to Kootenay Lake; the Kootenay and Arrowhead from Lardo to Trout Lake; and the extension of the Columbia and Western into the Kettle Valley, among others.

During this era of frenzied railway expansion, mushroom-ing communities and million dollar mines, sternwheelers were prominent. First was the *Lytton*, the C.K.S.N.'s $38,000 vessel, "built of the best material by the most experienced ship carpenters in Victoria." She left Revelstoke at 5 o'clock on July 2, 1890, with "hearty good wishes and . . . waving of handkerchiefs." At midnight "a grand display of thunder and lightning . . . greeted the steamboat, whose well tinned and painted decks shed the water like a canvasback." She would prove a successful and profitable vessel.

Another successful investment for the C.K.S.N. was the *Kootenai*. The firm bought her for $10,000 in promissary notes, a sum she dutifully paid off in her first few voyages. She also brought to four the sternwheelers operating on the river since Captain Sanderson had bought the *Marion* and shipped her overland from Golden to Revelstoke. But an

The Despatch, *below at Sproat's Landing, was the only twin-hulled sternwheeler to ply B.C. waters. The photo was taken by surveyor Dr. G. M. Dawson about 1889.*

ore discovery that became a legend made the four totally inadequate.

The legend was born the same month that the *Lytton* left on her maiden voyage. Two prospectors called at the Government office in Nelson to record claims on Red Mountain, some 50 miles to the southwest near the U.S. border. Since they had staked one more claim than the law permitted, they offered the extra to mining recorder E. S. Topping if he paid recording fees on all five. Topping, a former trapper, prospector, and frontiersman, quickly produced the necessary $12.50.

Assays from the claim tested high and Topping realized that the discovery was a major one. But as a veteran mining man he also knew that while discovering rich ore was one thing, getting it to a smelter was something else. But in the case of Red Mountain, this problem had solved itself. Six miles down Trail Creek Valley from Red Mountain was the Columbia River. Here the ore could be loaded aboard the new sternwheeler *Lytton* for shipment downstream to Little

Dalles where the recently completed Spokane Falls and Northern Railway provided access to a smelter.

That autumn, Topping sold sixteen-thirtieths of his claim, which he had named the LeRoi, for $16,000. Later, he sold the rest for $14,000, thus receiving $30,000 for his $12.50 investment. The LeRoi proved extremely rich, ultimately selling for $3 million. It and surrounding claims resulted in the birth of two communities, Trail and Rossland, and yielded 6 million tons of ore worth $125 million.

Stimulated by the massive ore discoveries and by an influx of U.S. residents bound for the prairies to take up free land, the West Kootenay flourished. To keep pace with this expansion, the C.K.S.N. ordered two new sternwheelers.

First was for service on Kootenay Lake. She was the *Nelson*, launched at Nelson June 11, 1891, the pioneer sternwheeler on Kootenay Lake. "The boat presents a handsome appearance," noted the local paper, the *Miner*, "and will take front rank among river steamers in British Columbia." She was a "most commodious vessel . . . staunchly built, while

Above: The Lytton *during construction of the road from Robson to Greenwood. The upper photo on the opposite page shows the* Nelson, *below her the* City of Ainsworth. *When the Nelson was launched the local paper reported that "Her lines were pronounced the finest of any boat on the inland waters of the North Pacific Coast."*

However, accommodation on early sternwheelers wasn't

always first class as a story told by veteran Captain Estabrooks emphasized. One passenger complained that mosquitoes were so bad he couldn't sleep. "Then why didn't you pull the covers over your head?" inquired a travelling companion.

"I did that," was the reply, "but the bedbugs were so bad I couldn't stand it."

every provision is made for the convenience of travellers ....." She was also colorful, with the dining and the ladies room white, boiler deck Prussian blue, and "Paris green trim on the eaves of the upper deck." Her assigned task was summarized in eight words: "Get all she could of Kootenay Lake trade."

The other addition to the C.K.S.N. fleet was the *Columbia*, a $74,000 vessel which had her hull built at Portland in sections then shipped by rail to Northport in Washington and put together by "twenty-five of the best ship carpenters on the coast." She left for Revelstoke on her maiden voyage on August 22, 1891, "a fine looking river vessel with first-class accommodation for about 40 passengers . . . comfortably furnished and equipped with machinery that will send her upstream a-flying."

On Kootenay Lake, meanwhile, the *Nelson* was joined by a second sternwheeler, the *Spokane*. She wasn't exactly a rival since her primary purpose was to aid construction of the Great Northern Railway to Bonners Ferry. The railway itself, however, was a different matter, especially from a C.P.R. outlook. It gave Kootenay Lake a direct connection with a transcontinental railway system whose aggressive president, James J. Hill, was determined to siphon traffic south to his line. He could also be expected to put his own sternwheelers on the lake, thus competing with the C.K.S.N.

Then the next year major ore discoveries in the Slocan district between Arrow and Kootenay Lakes further stoked C.P.R. and G.N.R. rivalry. Additional mines appeared overnight, with ore shipped to a new community called Nakusp on Upper Arrow Lake or now booming Kaslo on Kootenay Lake. The two communities became intense rivals, with the C.P.R. supporting Nakusp and the G.N.R. championing Kaslo. This rivalry intensified when the C.P.R. backed the Nakusp and Slocan Railway from Nakusp to another new mining community named Sandon. For its part the G.N. backed the Kaslo and Slocan, a line that tapped Sandon ore by way of Kaslo.

Each development added new sternwheelers. In November

1892 another joined the C.K.S.N.'s growing fleet. She was the *Illecillewaet,* a craft with not only the machinery from the now retired *Despatch* but also with a design equally unorthodox. She was little more than a steam scow with "a square stern, a square bow deck with overhang, a sturdy wheel at the stern, a cabin for the Captain, and the balance deck room."

Captain Troup intended to sail her where no other sternwheeler could venture. Two inches of water was ample, but if it did get shallow she skimmed along the bottom on her sheathed hull. As the *Kootenay Star* summarized: ". . . with a draught of only two or three inches she walks right over the sandbars without wetting them."

The same year a third sternwheeler appeared on Kootenay Lake. She was the *City of Ainsworth,* a modest vessel licensed to carry 50 passengers. She wasn't elaborate but was appreciated by residents of the more isolated communities on Kootenay Lake since they had learned that the C.K.N.S. tended to ignore them when business was good elsewhere. By September the *Ainsworth's* owners proudly advertised that she "leaves Kaslo for Nelson at 6:30 a.m. daily (Sunday excepted) calling at Ainsworth, Pilot Bay and Balfour."

During 1892 railway rivalry continued to flourish. From the Spokane Falls and Northern terminus at Northport a branch line, the Nelson and Fort Shepperd, was being built to Nelson. This extension was viewed with dismay by C.P.R. officials. The all-Canadian route from Vancouver to Nelson meant a trip of some 560 miles that involved travelling by train to Revelstoke, sternwheeler down the Arrow system to Sproat's Landing, then rail again to Nelson. The trip took 3 days under favorable conditions, much longer at other times. The new route from Nelson to Spokane, on the other hand, was only 180 miles with direct, year-round access.

To improve its service, in 1893 the C.P.R. started building a 27-mile spur section from Revelstoke to the head of Upper Arrow Lake, thus by-passing a troublesome section of the Columbia River. But now competition wasn't restricted to railways. It engulfed the sternwheelers and flourished among townsite promoters. During 1893, for instance, the *Nelson Miner* carried pages of glowing advertisements praising townsites such as Lardeau, Trout Lake City, Lardo, Duncan City, Argenta, Nelson, Sandon, Kaslo, Nakusp and many others.

For Lardeau, lots were on sale even though the townsite was no more than "arrangements have been made for a clearing of a portion of the Townsite, for the erection of hotels and stores. . . ."

The promoters of Trout Lake City modestly noted that their community "is going to be one of the richest mining regions in America" and hustled lots on the basis that "the owners intend to expend money on streets and other improvements in the spring."

A full page advertisement stressed the potential of Lardo. It was "gateway of the Lardo-Duncan mining camps, a railway point, the head of navigation at the north end of Kootenay Lake and the terminus of the Government trail to the mines."

The promoters, though, seemingly didn't believe their optimistic sales pitch. Lots were offered on the basis of ⅓ cash, ⅓ in 3 months, and full payment within 6 months.

While the boom brought prosperity to the Kootenay-Arrow country, it also brought to the C.K.S.N. its first serious challenge. Early in 1893 the Nelson and Bonners Ferry papers ran tantalizing news items about a new "flyer" being built at Bonners Ferry by the Kaslo Transportation Company. Its purpose was to "put the C.K.S.N. out of business."

To counter the threat, the C.K.S.N. bought the now inactive *Spokane* and spliced 30 feet to her. The result was "the most ungainly looking sternwheeler ever to ply on any water in southeastern B.C.," but it gave the firm two vessels to counter the looming competition. Unfortunately for the Kaslo Transportation Company and those who disliked the policies of both the C.P.R. and the C.K.S.N., the competition wasn't to prove serious.

On April 8 the *Kootenai Herald* at Bonners Ferry announced the launching of the new vessel, the *State of Idaho:* "A drizzling rain did not deter the many from at-

The upper photo shows the State of Idaho *surging up the Kootenay River towards Bonners Ferry. Above is a view of Baker Street in Nelson in 1897.*

tendance. At 5:00 p.m. amid the booming of explosives and the cheers of populace, the boat slipped down the greased skids into the water."

On May 6 she completed her maiden voyage to Kaslo, welcomed by the "booming of anvils and the wailing of brass bands." She made the trip in 10 hours, but a week later the *Nelson* clipped 13 minutes off this time. Unfortunately, the new "flyer" proved unable to match her newspaper publicity. Worse, as a paper later noted: "Fate has had, it would appear, her spite against her."

That September in a Wild West classic she sped down the Kootenay River to avoid seizure by an irate sheriff for back debts. She was then put on the Nelson-Kaslo run, but her career was short. At 4 a.m. on November 10 she rammed her bow into the rocky shore near Ainsworth.

The force of the crash twisted her cabin doors, trapping those inside until doors were battered in by deckhands. Passengers were fortunate for as the *Miner* reported ". . . that they lived . . . was due to a mere chance. When the

vessel struck her bow run up on a narrow shelf which held the hull fast. Her stern was hanging over 300 feet of water, and if the *Idaho* had struck ten feet to either side of the exact spot where she went on, in all probability she would have rebounded and settled immediately with all on board."

For one of her passengers, G. P. Alexander, the day proved even more eventful. For $350 he ended up owning the battered vessel. The strange sequence of events started when the original owners decided that the *State of Idaho* was a total loss. That afternoon they auctioned her "as is, where is," with Alexander the highest bidder. Later the unlucky vessel was towed to Kaslo for repairs and eventually returned to service.

During the period when the *State of Idaho* experienced

The Kootenay Lake communities of Ainsworth, below, and Kaslo, lower right, in 1897. Lower left shows Trail about 1895 when it was known as Trail Creek Landing.

"Fate's spite against her," the C.K.S.N. was also battered by fate. The *Columbia* burned up while loading wood about 6 miles south of Trail, a severe loss since the Arrow-Kootenay continued to flourish and every vessel was working to capacity.

Places that shortly before were a name and a clearing in the wilderness had grown into substantial communities. Kaslo was typical. It had a population of 3,000 and grew daily. "Boat after boat coming to Kaslo brought loads of men numbering from 125 to 150 a load," noted a booklet, *Historical Kaslo*. "Accommodation was at a premium. There were three men for every bed, so beds were used in shifts. Hotels were built in a month's time. The Slocan Hotel, one of Kaslo's finest, was constructed in 30 days with wet lumber, used as it was sawn. The hotel boasted 70 rooms and 75 carpenters were used in construction. When the timber dried out, there was little privacy in the hotel rooms."

But like most pioneer communities, Kaslo knew calamity as well as prosperity. On February 25, 1894 the lower half

of Front Street disappeared in a $100,000 fire. Less than four months later a vicious summer storm combined with a late spring flood to sweep away or damage beyond repair another $250,000 worth of buildings. Along with bridges and roads, the wharf washed out and the sternwheeler *Spokane* was made into a temporary landing place. She returned to service when the crisis ended but on March 21, 1895, caught fire at Kaslo and was destroyed.

Now only three vessels remained in the C.K.S.N. fleet: *Lytton* and *Kootenai* on Arrow Lakes and *Nelson* on Kootenay Lake. In May the latter vessel was given competition when the *State of Idaho*, renamed *Alberta*, started a regular service between Nelson and Kaslo.

The West Kootenay had now entered an era when smelters were nearly as prevalent as railways. By 1895 a $650,000

Main communities on the Upper Arrow system were Nakusp, below, and Revelstoke, at bottom. On the opposite page the Nakusp is shown "wooding up" on Lower Arrow Lake.

smelter was operational at Pilot Bay on the east shore of Kootenay Lake and a community of 1,000 grew around it. The same year construction started on another at Nelson plus one at Trail, while yet another had been built at Revelstoke.

To keep pace with booming conditions the C.K.S.N. launched a new sternwheeler at Nakusp on July 1, 1895. She was the *Nakusp,* a magnificient 171-foot vessel that could carry more freight than *Lytton* and *Kootenai* combined. She was easily the finest sternwheeler in the province, complete with hot and cold running water, steam heat and electric lights. Her dining room, richly decorated in white and gold, arched to a dome two decks high. Glittering chandeliers swung from the ornate ceiling while plants and flowers added additional splashes of color. The "floating palace" was an immediate success but she, too, would soon experience "fate's spite against her."

In December the C.K.S.N. lost the veteran *Kootenai* when she struck a rock in Upper Arrow Lake and settled in

about 4 feet of water. She was later towed to Nakusp but her planking had so deteriorated that she was dismantled.

To replace her, the Company launched a new sternwheeler at Nakusp on May 9, 1896. She was the *Trail,* designed basically for freighting and barge pushing. She was, nevertheless, warmly greeted when she arrived at Trail on her first voyage. As the *Trail Creek News* reported: "All the whistles in Trail made themselves heard when the . . . *City of Trail* came into town. . . . Everyman in town who could get away from his place of business was at the landing to meet the namesake of our embryo city, and the boat received an ovation."

Meanwhile, on Kootenay Lake the C.K.S.N. had added to its fleet "one of the most beautifully proportioned sternwheelers in the Pacific Northwest." She was the *Kokanee,* launched at Nelson on April 7. Of the launching the *Miner* reported: ". . . in all the bravery of flying colors, trim and coy, the debutante took her first plunge into the blue waves. The paper further noted that "It is doubtful if a

123

more graceful or better appointed boat can be found in British Columbia." Built for speed, she could reel off an easy 18 miles an hour.

To compete with her, the owners of the *Alberta* started work on a new vessel at Mirror Lake near Kaslo. As she grew so did speculation about the speed of the new "flyer." The *Kaslo Kootenian* observed on November 14 that the new vessel "has been almost the one topic of conversation in steamboat and travelling circles for some time and her debut is looked forward to . . . especially as much interest centers about her speed qualifications."

The new vessel, the *International*, was launched in November. "SHE IS A BEAUTY BRIGHT," noted the paper in a headline. "The appointments of the new ship are elegant," the news report continued, "and every care has been taken to promote comfort and please the eye of the many patrons of the line . . . ."

Unfortunately for Kaslo residents, her reputation "as a flyer" was unfounded since she had to struggle to maintain

15 miles an hour.

Nevertheless, she tested the *Kokanee* at any opportunity. On December 12, 1896, the *Kootenian* noted: "In a short race yesterday morning in the vicinity of Nelson, the steamer *International* outran the *Kokanee* by two lengths. The broom may now be shifted to another masthead. . . ."

Then occurred an event which temporarily replaced stern-wheel races as a newspaper topic. For $200,000 the C.P.R. bought out the pioneer C.K.S.N. Company.

Directors of the railway firm were undoubtedly influenced by the fact that in the West Kootenay they were losing the competitive battle to the U.S. railways, the Great Northern and the Spokane Falls and Northern, both of which offered shorter routes to market than the C.P.R. The move proved very effective for it eventually won for the Canadian firm complete control of the Arrow Lakes and both West and East Kootenay. It also resulted in several majestic stern-wheelers appearing on Arrow and Kootenay Lakes.

First was the *Kootenay*, launched at Nakusp in April 1897,

The Trail, above, was basically a freighter but the Kokanee, upper right, was a sleek, speedy vessel. At right is the Bonnington on the ways at Nakusp shortly before her launching. On the opposite page is a menu from the Kootenay. It was then legal to sell game meat, hence venison cutlets are featured as one of the meat courses.

During the sternwheel era, a few propeller-driven vessels also operated on the Kootenay-Arrow system. The William Hunter, for instance, was the first steam-powered vessel on Slocan Lake. Her boiler, two propellers, and other ironware were brought by packhorse over a rough mountain trail from Nakusp. All lumber was sawn by hand. She was, as one resident summarized, "hand-hewn and homemade." Nevertheless she received the traditional launching with "drinks and cigars liberally supplied by the owners . . . ." Later, she was to have an unusual experience. One trip as she left the dock those on board crowded to one side as they bid friends adieu. The weight so unbalanced her that she promptly rolled over, dunking but not drowning any of her surprised passengers.

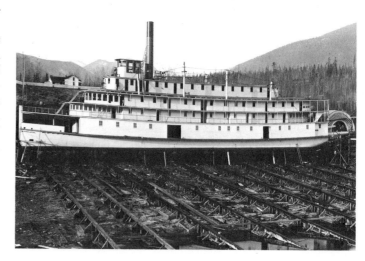

"a big sternwheeler with wide decks, comfortable cabins and first rate meals." In June with the *Nakusp* she commenced a daily service between Arrowhead and Trail. Business was brisk, for as the *Trail Creek Times* noted: "The C.P.R. steamer *Kootenay* has worn out two clotheslines this year in running up flags in honor of distinguished men who have neglected their business affairs at home long enough to pay Trail a visit."

Two other sternwheelers that joined the C.P.R. fleet in 1897 were the 155-foot-long *Slocan* launched at Rosebery for service on Slocan Lake and the *Rossland*. The latter was built at Nakusp and joined the Arrow Lakes service on November 18. Designed to make the 256-mile trip from Arrowhead to Robson and return in a day, she was a "real flyer" whose engines drove her faster than the ocean liners of the day.

During the same year the veteran *Marion* embarked on another overland journey. A C.P.R. subsidiary, the Kootenay and Arrowhead Railway, announced it was building a line up the Lardeau River from the north end of Kootenay Lake to Upper Arrow Lake. Then the G.N.R. through a subsidiary, the Kaslo, Lardo-Duncan, began a survey up the other side of the river. To capitalize on these projects, Captain Sanderson again made history by shipping his well travelled sternwheeler by rail from Arrow to Kootenay Lake.

The *Lytton* also completed a historic voyage in 1897. Now in her 7th successful season, she became the first vessel to retrace the route above Revelstoke first plied by the *Forty-Nine* in 1865. Although she had engines far superior to those in the pioneer vessel, she was 6 hours fighting through Little Dalles Rapids. On the return trip, timed with a stop watch, she rocketed through in 6 minutes, 51 seconds.

A few months later the *Nakusp* made headlines of a different nature. On December 24 she caught fire at Arrowhead and burned to the waterline. While the loss of this outstanding vessel was a setback to the C.P.R., it didn't deter the railway company from its plan to beat out its U.S. rivals. On January 28, 1898 it purchased the Trail smelter and the Columbia and Western Railway for $1 million. It was another coup since the smelter was to outlast all others, grow into the world's largest lead-zinc complex and return $1,000 for every $1 invested.

Railway rivalry, however, still flourished. In an excellent unpublished manuscript, *Sternwheelers - Sandbars and Switchbacks,* Kootenay historian Edward L. Affleck captured the hetic duel when he wrote:

"The struggle for supremacy between the C.P.R. and the G.N.R. carried on in earnest throughout 1898. Galvanized into activity by the threat of the G.N.R. extension from Bonner's Ferry to Kuskanook, the C.P.R. at last forged ahead with the construction of the B.C. Southern Rry. west from the Crow's Nest Pass . . . and steel was pushed through to the shores of Kootenay Lake by November, 1898. During the summer of 1898, slips to accommodate 15-car barges were built at Nelson and at Kootenay Landing, the transfer point at the south head of Kootenay Lake above Kuskanook.

"The G.N.R. countered the C.P.R.'s move with two master strokes. First, the three Corbin lines, viz. the Spokane Falls & Northern, the Nelson & Fort Shepperd, and the Red Mountain Railways, were purchased. In addition, the Kootenay Railway and Navigation Co. was organized to buy up the Kaslo & Slocan Rry., the International Navigation & Trading Co., the Bedlington & Nelson Rry., the Kootenai Valley Rry., and the Kaslo and Lardo-Duncan Rry. Construction on the Kootenai Valley Rry. and Bedlington & Nelson Rry. started on Nov. 26 1898, and was scheduled to reach Kuskanook the following July. Plans were also drawn up for the extension of the Bedlington & Nelson Rry. up to the east side of the Main Lake of Kootenay Lake to connect with the Kaslo & Lardo-Duncan line at Argenta."

Among new sternwheelers launched during the 1898 struggle between the C.P.R. and the G.N.R. were the *Victoria* for service on Trout Lake and the *Minto* and the *Moyie,* two vessels still remembered with affection by Arrow and Kootenay Lake pioneers.

The pair, prefabricated in sections at Toronto, were originally intended for service on the Stikine River as part of an "all-Canadian" water-railway route to the Klondike gold fields. When the projected railway never materialized the vessels were diverted to Arrow and Kootenay Lakes.

S. S. Kootenay

CANADIAN PACIFIC RAILWAY COMPANY

Supper ▦ Dec 6th 1899

Soup
Consommé de Boeuf clair

Fish
Broiled Finnon Haddock, Fried Olympia Oysters

Broiled
Chicken on Toast
Kidney + Bacon
Venison Cutlets with Jelly
Lamb Chops
Sirloin + Tenderloin Steaks
Mushroom Sauce

Cold Meats
Roast Beef
Turkey
Ham
Corned Ox Tongue

Potatoes
Baked, Saratoga, Lyonaise
Chicken Salad

Hot Bread
Parker House Rolls

Cheese, Dressed Celery

Preserves
Peaches with Cream, Strawberrys
Jam Marmalade
Assorted Cakes

Fruit

Tea.   Coffee.

The first, the *Moyie*, was launched at Nelson on October 22, with the *Nelson Miner* reporting: "Mrs. Troup broke a bottle of champagne over the bows in the most approved fashion, the ropes were cut, the newly christened *Moyie* slid rapidly and safely down the ways, and, in much less time than it takes to write it, she was slowly and gracefully on the water with her steam up and everything ready for her trial trip.

"About an hour afterwards the steamer made a trial run up to 5-Mile Point and gave every satisfaction to those in charge of her. She is not quite so fast as the *Kokanee* but can make her 16 knots an hour."

Her maiden voyage was December 7, an all-star event to inaugurate passenger service on the new B.C. Southern Railway from Alberta to Kootenay Lake. Aboard were newspapermen, railway officials, mayors and similar dignitaries from communities such as Rossland, Trail, Robson, Kaslo, Sandon, Nelson and other district points. The *Moyie* was to serve three generations of Kootenay residents,

become the last active commercial sternwheeler in B.C. and the only one preserved in operating condition.

Her sister, the *Minto*, was launched at Nakusp on November 19. Named after Canada's Governor-General, she was 162 feet long with accommodation for 70 passengers. Like the *Moyie* she had a composite wood and steel hull and was also to record a distinguished career. Fifty-six years later when her red paddlewheel finally stilled she had travelled over 2 million miles serving isolated communities along the mountain-flanked Arrow Lakes.

Ten days after the *Minto* was launched, the Arrow Lakes-Kootenay region was saddened by its worst sternwheel disaster. On November 29 the *City of Ainsworth* left Nelson for Bonners Ferry but got caught in a gale. Eight cords of firewood on her bow made her sluggish and she began to ship water. Passengers and crew hurriedly tossed the cordwood overboard but this created a new problem. The lightened bow rose and water on board ran aft, causing her to settle by the stern. Her paddlewheel virtually stopped and

The Kokanee and the Kuskanook race down Kootenay Lake in 1908. The top photo on the opposite page shows the Kootenay on Upper Arrow Lake about 1912, while the bottom photo is of the Slocan which plied Slocan Lake, a waterway between Arrow and Kootenay Lakes.
Since sternwheelers were the only method of transportation

to many pioneer communities, residents often claimed they could hear a sternwheeler's whistle further than they could see the northern lights. While the distance was possibly exaggerated, isolated trappers and prospectors awaiting supplies, especially bottled goods from "the government store," swore they could hear the whistle for 20 miles.

she swung broadside to the waves. She lurched to port then to starboard, each roll worse than the preceding one. Then she heeled over so far that water poured into her smokestack.

When she began to wallow, First Officer Perrier launched a small lifeboat but it swamped. Four of the five aboard vanished into the snow-lashed waves. Then Captain Lean and some crew members launched the other lifeboat. As it bobbed beside the smokestack Captain Lean shouted "I want three more men." Some passengers rushed to get aboard and it capsized. Five more people vanished into the storm.

The lifeboat was dragged back aboard but the oars had washed away. Pilothouse door and ladder were smashed for paddles and Captain Lean, seaman Donnelly and engineer W. J. Kane bailed out the lifeboat with their hats. Then the three took aboard four passengers and rowed some two miles to shore. Twice more they undertook the treacherous trip to rescue those still surviving. Final death roll in the mishap was two passengers and seven crew.

The battered sternwheeler ultimately washed on to the rocks at the entrance to Crawford Bay but later sank in 100 feet of water while the tug *Kaslo* was towing her to Pilot Bay.

Loss of the veteran *Ainsworth* left five sternwheelers on Kootenay Lake but in February 1900 a new vessel joined them. She was the *Argenta*, a small vessel built at Mirror Lake near Kaslo by the Kootenay Railway and Navigation Co., a subsidiary of the Great Northern Railway. She was intended for shallow-water service at the north end of Kootenay Lake and on Duncan River and Duncan Lake.

Then in September the Kootenay Railway and Navigation Co. launched a sternwheeler designed specifically to compete with the C.P.R. She was the *Kaslo,* largest and finest vessel yet to appear on Kootenay Lake. A feature of the vessel was an "alcove dining room, affording passengers a perfect view of the passing scenery while at the table." All staterooms had "fixed basins and are supplied with taps," while the interior decorations "are carved mahogany and mirror plate. The transoms are in ground glass relieved with photographic transparencies of choice local scenes."

With her and a new rail connection between Bonners Ferry and Kuskanook, the G.N. intended to whack the C.P.R. with tough body blows. Unfortunately for the G.N., expected traffic didn't materialize. Instead of staggering the now solidly entrenched Canadian firm, the G.N. found itself in trouble. Next year it abandoned most of its Kootenay Lake service, a preliminary move in what became a complete withdrawal from the region.

During this period four veteran sternwheelers joined the ranks of the vanished: the *Marion* was retired, the *Illecillewaet* sold for use as a barge, the hard-working *Lytton* beached above Robson, while the *Trail* had burned up.

One new vessel appeared. She was the *Revelstoke*, launched at Nakusp on January 10, 1902. Her owners, Revelstoke businessmen, intended to use her on some 40 miles of dangerous waters of the Columbia River between Revelstoke and Death Rapids—the region that attracted the *Forty-Nine* upstream nearly forty years previously.

The *Revelstoke* was a sleek, 125-foot vessel especially designed for turbulent water. Unloaded she drew only 22 inches and her engines developed over double the power of any of her predecessors. Although the Big Bend gold fields had long been exhausted her owners hoped to tap a new source of riches—the area's forests. Under Captain A. Forslund and engineer H. Colbeck she served 13 successful seasons on the tricky waterway, her passengers and cargo varying from loggers to sawmill equipment, from optimistic prospectors who refused to believe that the area was "played out" to machinery for the mines which like spring flowers bloomed and faded.

After the *Revelstoke* entered service there was a 4-year lull when no new vessels joined the Arrow-Kootenay fleet. Then in 1906 the C.P.R. began an era of "super sternwheelers." First was the magnificent *Kuskanook.* She was prefabricated in the East and assembled at Nelson, a massive 1,008-ton vessel launched May 5, 1906. A civic holiday was declared and the *Victoria Colonist* recorded that the

Upper left shows the Victoria *on Trout Lake and, below it, the* Nelson *at the railway siding near Procter. On the facing page the* Rossland *churns down the Arrow Lakes.*

$150,000 vessel "was successfully christened and launched . . . in the presence of 3,500 people. . . ."

She made her first trip on July 8 when she took 300 passengers on an excursion across the lake. She proved the fastest vessel yet to appear, clipping off an easy 22 miles an hour. Her first test was July 12 when she raced the *Kaslo*. As the *Nelson Daily News* reported: "The new C.P.R. flyer *Kuskanook* had a little race last evening with the *Kaslo* while en route to Procter with the excursion. Nearing Busk's ranch, the *Kaslo* was sighted at a landing and she got away with a lead of about a quarter of a mile on the excursion boat. However, more coal was shovelled in and the engineer let out his engines with the result that the rival boat was quickly overhauled. . . ."

The next vessel to join the C.P.R.'s fleet was the largest sternwheeler yet to appear in B.C. waters and the biggest north of San Francisco. She was the 1,700-ton *Bonnington*, launched at Nakusp on April 24, 1911 for service on Arrow Lakes. Officials at Nakusp declared a half-day holiday and

with "myriad streamers fluttering and her enamel white sides gay with bunting . . . the first steel steamer of the C.P.R. interior service glided, with scarcely a tremor, down the greased ways of the local shipyard and gracefully kissed the waters of Arrow Lake."

The $160,000 vessel was " a remarkably handsome boat, with her graceful lines and her four decks. Her frame is of coast fir, while the finishing has been done in cedar. Her prevailing color above the water line is white, but in the interior finishing various tints are employed for trimmings."

The majestic vessel was part of a long range plan by the C.P.R. to develop the West Kootenay region into a major tourist center, complementing the Company's program for the Canadian Rockies. As part of the project a resort hotel was opened at Balfour on Kootenay Lake, then in 1913 a new ship was built for service on the lake.

She was the 1,869-ton *Nasookin,* largest sternwheeler ever to ply B.C. waters. Her hull was prefabricated at Port Arthur and assembled at the C.P.R. shipyard at Nelson. On April 30

"gaily decorated with flags and bunting she glided gracefully and majestically into the waters of Kootenay Lake to the accompaniment of a din of whistles which drowned the cheering of the crowd. . . ."

She was licensed to carry 550 passengers with comforts ranging from "a commodious dining room with a lofty ceiling" to promenade decks "all lighted by electricity." Of her the *Nelson Daily News* commented: "That the *Nasookin* may have a long and prosperous career should be the wish of every resident of Nelson. Her success means much to this city as well as to Kootenay and the Boundary generally. Her construction is a declaration by the Canadian Pacific railway of faith in this country and of its intention to develop its lines through this section as a tourist and passenger route."

Unfortunately, the C.P.R.'s plans for the future died during the First World War. The hotel at Balfour closed and neither the *Bonnington* nor the *Nasookin* fulfilled its intended purpose. Then in 1915 the C.P.R. completed a rail link from the Kettle Valley via Penticton to Princeton and the Coquihalla Canyon to its trans-continental line at Hope. For the first time the Arrow-Kootenay Lakes district had a direct, all-Canadian railway to the coast. For the sternwheelers, an era was closing. On Arrow Lakes service was reduced from daily to three trips northbound and three southbound a week, and the mighty *Bonnington* semi-retired.

By now many familiar vessels were gone. In 1910 the *Kaslo* ran aground and never again entered service. On July 16, 1914 the *Nelson* was burnt as part of a waterfront carnival at Nelson. Other vessels had a less colorful end.

The *International* became a bunkhouse at Riondel while the *Revelstoke* burned in a giant fire at Comaplix. The *Rossland* foundered in a heavy snowstorm at her moorings in Naskusp; in 1919 pioneer Captain Sanderson bought the *Kootenay* for use as a houseboat; and in 1923 the *Kokanee* was sold for a hunting and fishing lodge. Now remained only the *Nasookin*, *Kuskanook* and *Moyie* on Kootenay Lake; the *Bonnington* and *Minto* on the Arrow Lakes. But as new roads fingered along lake and river shore they, too, became surplus. In 1930 with the completion of the B.C. Southern rail link between Kootenay Landing and Procter, the *Nasookin* and the *Kuskanook* made their last scheduled runs and next year the *Bonnington* was retired. The *Nasookin*, however, started a new career. She was rented, then purchased, by the B.C. Government for use as a vehicle ferry across Kootenay Lake, a service she performed until 1946. She was tied up at Nelson and for several years used for training sea cadets, leaving only the two aging sister ships, *Minto* and *Moyie*. Then they were gone.

On April 24, 1954 the *Minto* backed from the wharf at West Robson on Lower Arrow Lake for the last time. Although her flags and bunting snapped bravely in the breeze,

The photo on the opposite page shows the difference in size of the Rossland *and* Minto *compared with the stately* Bonnington, *built especially for the tourist trade.*
At upper left the Revelstoke *is at St. Leon with an excursion party, August 25, 1909. At center is the* Argenta *at Healy's Landing in the late 1890's while opposite the* Kaslo *loads ore. The* Revelstoke *served mostly on the Columbia River from Revelstoke to La Porte. Bucking the current on the 42-mile upstream journey she burned 42 cords of wood; riding the river back, 1 cord.*

sorrow was the general mood of Captain Bob Manning, some 150 passengers and residents of communities she served for 56 years.

At such familiar ports-of-call as Syringa Creek, Deer Park, Renata, Broadwater, Edgewood, Fauquier, Needles, Burton, Carroll's Landing, Graham's Landing, Arrow Park and others, residents waited to pay respect to their faithful friend.

At Edgewood a tearful crowd sang *Auld Lang Syne* while on the beach Jock Ford piped a lament. At Burton, citizens placed a large wreath on her weather-worn bow and at Arrowhead farmer John Nelson greeted her with an enormous sign: "Let us honor the brave pioneers of navigation on the scenic Arrow Lakes by making it possible to continue the very efficient services of the S.S. *Minto.*"

At Halcyon Hot Springs a lonely figure in army uniform waited patiently, across his chest 17 decorations awarded him by European governments during the First World War. He was Brigadier-General F. W. Burnham who in 1924 had built a sanitarium at Halcyon where he continued his service to the sick and crippled.

The *Minto* docked and Captain Manning came down from the wheelhouse to greet the 82-year-old doctor-general. Radio and press reporters interviewed the distinguished humanitarian for the last time, then the *Minto* was underway again, responding in a hoarse whistle to the general's farewell salute.

Last call for the *Minto* was St. Leon Hot Springs. Here a three-storied, weathered hotel stood in the trees above the beach. Built in 1901 by a pioneer prospector named Mike Grady, it had a brief career then he closed its doors to live the life of a recluse. For years he met every boat, a storybook character with flowing curly hair, flourishing mustache and a pet cougar. But the *Minto* had outlasted him by 10 years. With a whistle blast to his memory she pulled from the shore and continued to Nakusp. For the last time she nosed into the wharf and the welcoming crowd watched the paddlewheel slow down then stop.

At first it appeared that she would be preserved as a museum. The C.P.R. sold her to Nakusp for $1 but residents quickly lost interest. In April 1956 she was sold to a Nelson junk firm for $750. Soon they had stripped furnishings, boilers, engines, paddlewheel—everything but the hull.

On his farm up the lake at Galena Bay, John Nelson heard the news and decided that if townspeople in Nakusp wouldn't save her he would. With $800 of his slim life savings he bought the remnants of the vessel, had her towed across the lake and beached on his farm. Unfortunately the reprieve was temporary. Because of his age and limited resources, John Nelson could do little to restore the vessel, a project estimated to cost $100,000. Then on November 26, 1967, the 88-year-old pioneer died. On August 1, 1968, so did the remains of the *Minto*.

Three years previously, work started on the Columbia River Basin Development. As part of the project a 170-foot-high dam at the outlet of the Arrow Lakes turned the picturesque route once plied by the sternwheelers into a 200-square-mile reservoir. Many communities and farms once served by the *Minto* disappeared under water up to 40 feet deep, among them her last resting place. On August 1, 1968 the hulk was towed onto the lake where Walter Nelson struck the match to provide a Viking's funeral for his father's dream. Grey smoke and red heat towered into the blue sky, within minutes reducing to charred remnants a famous landmark.

Meanwhile, on Kootenay Lake the *Moyie* had been more fortunate. Her last run was April 27, 1957 and, like that of her sister, a sad occasion for scores of lake-side residents. She maintained her regular schedule, calling at such familiar places as Queens Bay, Kootenay Landing, Walkers Landing, Riondel, Ainsworth, Mirror Lake, Kaslo, Birchdale, Johnsons Landing, Lardeau, and Argenta.

At Lardeau a banner read "Farewell *Moyie*." At Argenta residents presented her with a wreath and as she left the strains of *Auld Lang Syne* followed her foaming wake. She received a daffodil wreath at Johnson's Landing, while at

The Minto on Lower Arrow Lake in early winter during the last years of her career. Those on board for her last voyage included Mrs. O. M. Maitland who made her first trip on the vessel 55 years before.

Opposite: The Viking's funeral for the Minto on Upper Arrow Lake in August 1968, photographed by G. P. James. She had faithfully served pioneer residents for over half a century, but faster transportation methods made her fate inevitable.

Kaslo stores were closed and a uniformed band met her at the wharf. Red, white and blue bunting decorated dock pilings and a sign stated: "Better Lo'ed Ye Ne'er Will Be. Will Ye No Come Back Again?"

The *Moyie* completed her 87-mile voyage in 9 hours, then with a farewell blast of her whistle slid into the wharf at Procter. She had served just a few months short of 60 years.

Fortunately, she was not to suffer the indignity of the *Minto*. Although Kaslo had dwindled from the once flourishing gateway to the Slocan district to a village of 700, residents felt that their community should be the *Moyie's* final home. The C.P.R. agreed and gave her to the village. To supervise the formidable task of upkeep and management the Kootenay Lake Historical Society was formed. Its first president was Noel Bacchus, a trapper and rancher who had forsaken a London banking career for the freedom of Kootenay Lake. His enthusiasm, supported by the Board of Trade, Service Clubs, Fire Brigade and scores of residents, resulted in $15,000 being raised to finance the first phase of the preservation project.

Today the *Moyie* rests in a concrete berth at the end of Front Street in Kaslo. She is preserved as she was on her last trip and the policy of the Historical Society is to change nothing that will alter her appearance. Wheelhouse, galley, boilers and engines are intact and in place, even the varying tones of her whistles are preserved on a recording.

Since Kaslo is off the main highway the *Moyie* was comparatively lonely during her first years on display. But British Columbians have a glowing pride in their colorful history and she now welcomes over 10,000 people a year. In her white hull, buff funnel and red paddlewheel she is a proud symbol of an era known to fewer and fewer people. One of those people, the late Captain James Fitzsimmons, captured the flavor of the period when he described it as days "of whitewater runs and forced steam; of snags, sweepers, sand and gravel bars; of rocks, ripples, low water, ice-bridges, and all the romance and urge of the great river business in the days of Kootenay in the making."

CHAPTER TEN

Northern B.C. and Yukon

The Yukon River is one of North America's major waterways. Born only 15 miles from the Pacific Ocean in the jagged Coast Mountains where the northwestern tip of British Columbia joins Alaska and Yukon, she flows 2,100 miles—give or take a few—before reaching salt water at Norton Sound in the Bering Sea. On this journey she drains 330,000 square miles—larger than the combined area of California, Oregon and Washington. With silt from this massive basin she has created a delta upwards of 80 miles across, a treeless expanse where sky and horizon merge in a grey line, where water is generally shallow enough to wade and where 40 miles from shore is still only 10 feet deep. Since only one main channel threads the delta's intertwined maze of shallows and islands, during the paddlewheel era stranded sternwheelers became a common landmark.

From headwater streams and lakes the Yukon flows roughly north-northwest for some 850 miles to cross into the Arctic Circle, then turns and for 1,250 miles flows southwestward to tidewater. Five hundred miles upstream she is still over a mile wide, six or more where her channels wander into the Arctic tundra. This bleak, flat land, home of the Eskimo, the white fox, snowy owl and polar bear, is a stark contrast to the colorful route through the enormous interior of Alaska and Yukon.

Here a green mantle of spruce and lodgepole pine, aspen and willow covers the hills, while snow-capped peaks form an impressive backdrop. Moose, wolves, grizzly, caribou, white Dall sheep and other wildlife flourish. Tangles of pink roses, sweeping strokes of magenta fireweed, bluebells, snowy mountain avens, and wild sweetpeas in hues of lavender to red add splashes of color everywhere. Raspberries, strawberries, blueberries and cranberries spread by the mile while in tens of thousands of sloughs and backwaters, geese, ducks and other waterfowl nest by the millions.

The Clifford Sifton shooting Miles Canyon Rapids on the Yukon River, July 24, 1900. Once through the Canyon, the sternwheelers could not return upstream. For this reason, Whitehorse at the lower end of Miles Canyon-Whitehorse Rapids became head of navigation on the Yukon River.

But while summer is idyllic, it is short. In a good year navigation season is about four months—mid-June to mid-October. The river can freeze solid overnight and vessels caught in this icy embrace risk destruction during break-up the following May or June.

The ice carries everything before it—a ponderous battering ram that can be heard 15 miles away. William Ogilvie, a Canadian Government surveyor sent to the Yukon in 1887, watched a block of ice four feet thick standing on edge in water 45 feet deep rolling like an immense wheel. During break-up the ice moves about 100 miles a day, crunching over or levering aside all obstacles. This massive fist of destruction claimed many sternwheelers, including three of the four pioneer vessels on the river.

One was the *New Racket*. In 1897 she was laid up for the winter in what was considered a protected backwater four miles above the trading post at Pelly on the Yukon River. Next spring at break-up she was being overhauled. In the H. W. McCurdy *Marine History of the Pacific Northwest*

one of the workmen related her fate: "The boat was just clear of the water when the main Yukon ice broke and jammed on an island about three miles below the post. The water in the slough rose 20 feet inside of five minutes, lifted Mr. *New Racket* up and landed it back in the timber about a quarter of a mile, where it landed gracefully on top of a stump which penetrated the bottom of the boat, and as far as I know she is there yet."

The crushing power of Yukon ice was accorded the greatest respect by sternwheel captains. For instance, during the gold rush Captain W. P. Gray was bound upstream on the last trip of the season with the *Robert Kerr*, her cargo $100,000 in meat and vegetables for Dawson City. About 350 miles from Dawson a main shaft broke. "A steamboat under command of my brother, Capt. Jas. T. Gray, came down with the officers of the A. E. Co. and the crews of three other steamboats aboard that had been laid up at Dawson for the winter," he wrote. "We offered the president of the Alaska Exploration Co. $50,000 if they would tow

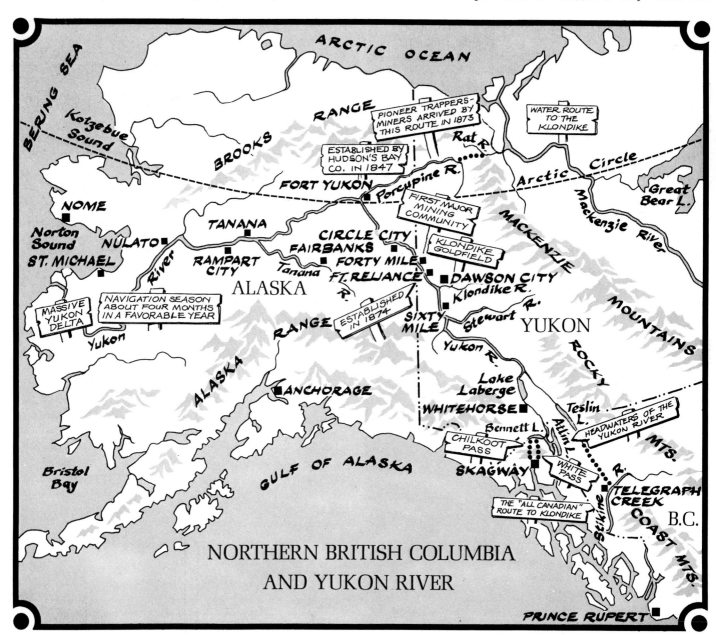

NORTHERN BRITISH COLUMBIA
AND YUKON RIVER

the *Robert Kerr* to Dawson. He refused as the ice was too close . . . ."

In an outstanding feat of engineering the *Robert Kerr's* crew temporarily repaired the shaft and limped upstream. As they got closer to Dawson, Captain Gray offered another vessel $10,000 to tow them the rest of the way. It was refused, "as they were afraid of the ice."

Sternwheel days opened on the Yukon River in 1869 and ended 86 years later in 1955. Nowhere else in North America did the flat-bottomed vessels play so important a part in both pioneer and modern transportation; nowhere else in Canada did so many appear on one river. Yukon historian W. D. MacBride compiled a list of some 250 vessels that plied the Yukon, most of them sternwheelers.

For crews and vessels, the Yukon provided a host of new experiences. Because of the shallow, ever-changing delta, the nearest port is St. Michael, 70 miles northward through the stormy Bering Sea. Even this haven is little better than open water since it is built on a low volcanic island with mud flats that prohibit ocean-going vessels from coming within two miles of its wharves.

For the first 400 miles or so upstream through the flat tundra country, driftwood provided the only fuel. It lined the shores in knotted windrows and covered sandbars in tangled heaps, some 40 or more feet high. But the wood, while plentiful, wasn't necessarily easy to gather. Because of shallow water vessels often couldn't get close to it, then crews frequently battled mosquitoes in such numbers that all who experienced them agreed "no adjective can exaggerate the discomfort and even torture provided by these pests."

Of all annoyances, however, the delta was the worst. Here impatient skippers spent hours, days and weeks stuck in the sand, while passengers frequently walked around the hull without getting their feet wet. One sternwheeler spent 30 hours in the sand even though she was five miles offshore and needed only four feet of water. The delta "breaks up in a labyrinth of blind, misleading channels, sloughs and swamps which extend over an immense territory with a most mournful and distressing prospect," wrote William Haskell in his book *Two Years in the Klondike and Alaska Goldfields*. "The country itself is scarcely above the level of the tides, and is covered with a monotonous cloak of scrubby willows and rank sedges. It is . . . a vast inland sea, filled with thousands and thousands of swale islets scarcely peeping above the surface."

The first sternwheeler to challenge the delta was the *Yukon*. On July 4, 1869, she left St. Michael with "flags flying and guns firing." A few hours later the pioneer voyage temporarily halted when she rammed a sandbar in the delta and was a day struggling free, even though she drew only 15 inches of water. The modest vessel was owned by the Alaska Commercial Co., brought north to better enable the firm to compete with the Hudson's Bay Company.

This famous fur-trading company had established itself in the Yukon 27 years earlier when a company clerk, Robert Campbell, built a post at Frances Lake. In 1846 he established another on the Pelly River and in 1847 another H.B.C. clerk, A. S. Murray, built Fort Yukon at the junction of the Porcupine and Yukon Rivers. Then in 1848 Campbell established a fourth post, Fort Selkirk at the junction of the Pelly and Lewes Rivers. In 1852 he left the Yukon, undertaking an incredible winter journey on snowshoes through some 3,000 miles of virtually uninhabited wilderness to Montreal.

Campbell and other fur traders knew that there was gold in the Yukon but they kept it a secret. They wanted furs, not gold. But over a 20-year period rumours filtered out and in 1873 two parties of trapper-prospectors arrived at Fort Yukon after a year-long trip that took them through British Columbia to the Mackenzie River and finally over the mountains near the Arctic Ocean to the Yukon watershed. Included were Frederick W. Hart, Arthur Harper, L. N. (Jack) McQuesten and Alfred H. Mayo. Next year the four joined the Alaska Commercial Co. as traders, but remained free to prospect as time permitted. In one form or another the arrangement lasted for over 20 years, during which time the four became the best known men in the Yukon.

Once moose were so plentiful along the Yukon that herds swam the river. The above drawing was done in 1883 and shows the sternwheeler Yukon amidst a herd of the animals. The same year, Frederick Schwatka explored the entire river and wrote that the pioneer paddlewheeler "could hardly make a voyage to old Fort Yukon and back without encountering a few herds of these animals swimming across the stream, and exciting were the bouts with them, often ending in victory for the moose with the Yukon aground on a bar of sand or gravel." Afterward the moose virtually disappeared, believed wiped out by a severe winter.

McQuesten's first assignment was to establish a trading post some 350 miles upstream from Fort Yukon, or about 1,600 miles from the mouth of the Yukon. Three tons of merchandise was stowed aboard the *Yukon* and with a whale boat in tow, she started upstream. She arrived in August 1874 and McQuesten established a post which he called Fort Reliance, about 6 miles upstream from where a river the Indians called the "Thron-diuck" flowed into the Yukon. At the junction of the Thron-diuck and Yukon was a triangle of creek-studded hills that pioneer miners would contemptuously call the "moose pasture" since they felt its only value was a source of winter meat. Ironically, its gravel contained about a quarter billion dollars in gold but not until an Indian shot a moose was its wealth accidently discovered. The Thron-diuck, or Tron-Deg as pioneer miners called it, then burst upon the world as the "Klondike."

But that was 22 years in the future. In the meantime Harper, Mayo and McQuesten continued trading and prospecting, with McQuesten even becoming a sternwheel captain. In summer he freighted supplies with the *Yukon*, often the only white man on board. "It is a wonder to me that we didn't blow her up or sink her as I didn't know anything about steam boating," he wrote. "Often we would get a moose in the water and all hands would grab the guns and let the steamer take care of herself . . . ."

The pioneer vessel, nevertheless, served until she was demolished by ice in the spring of 1880. She was the first claimed by the fearsome break-up; she wouldn't be the last.

The second sternwheeler on the river was the *St. Michael*, owned by the Western Fur and Trading Co. By 1879 she was making regular trips upstream under Captain P. M. Anderson. In 1882, the third appeared. She was the *New Racket*, a vessel "about forty feet long by about nine or

The Arctic, *below, in October 1896 became the first vessel to call at newly established Dawson City, staked by pioneer trader, Joe Ladue. The lower photo shows Ladue's house at Ogilvie on the Yukon River in 1895.*

ten feet wide . . . wholly taken up with engine and boiler." Her owner, prospector Edward Scheiffelin, had struck it rich in Arizona but after less than a year decided that hopes of finding gold in the Yukon "were too poor to justify my sojourn any longer . . . ."

The *New Racket* was bought by Harper, Mayo and McQuesten, with Mayo now becoming a skipper. While the vessel wasn't big, she was adaptable. In 1886 some miners hired her, disconnected engines from the paddlewheel and hooked them to pumps to provide water for their sluice boxes. In less than a month they cleared $1,000 each.

In 1889 the A.C. Co. launched the *Arctic*, first major sternwheeler to appear on the Yukon. The 125-foot vessel proved a most capable craft. Under Captain W. D. Moore in the season of 1895 alone she logged 14,000 miles in just over two months. "This has never, as far as I have learned, been repeated," commented W. Ogilvie in his book *Early Days on the Yukon*. The route "was over a course then but little known, where the pilot's memory was his only

chart, and that chart included more than 1,500 miles of tortuous channel—a channel varying with each shower of rain . . . ."

The *Arctic* changed the life pattern of some 300 miners who had by now drifted into the Yukon. Previously the *New Racket* and the *St. Michael* had been unable to carry sufficient supplies upstream for them to remain all winter. Many had to "go out," but now all who wished could stay. Most were around a settlement called Fortymile, established after an 1886 gold strike on the Fortymile River, a Yukon tributary 40 miles downstream from Fort Reliance. By 1890, Fortymile was the largest community on the entire 2,100-mile Yukon River. It consisted of 200 log cabins, six saloons, two blacksmith shops and other business places, including an opera house staffed by San Francisco dance-hall girls.

In 1893 another gold discovery on Birch Creek, a Yukon tributary some 140 miles downstream from Fortymile in Alaska, resulted in the birth of Circle City. By 1894 it had a log-cabin population of 500, served by 27 saloons.

The gradually expanding population along the Yukon resulted in the appearance of three additional sternwheelers. First was the *Portus B. Weare,* a 175-foot vessel built for a new firm, North American Transportation and Trading Company. In 1895 the A.C. Co. added two new vessels, the *Alice* and the *Bella.* Four major-sized sternwheelers now plied the river, but they were about to be overwhelmed by events in the "moose pasture."

One of the principals was George Washington Carmack, an American who lived with the Indians; the other was Robert Henderson, a veteran Canadian prospector who arrived in the Yukon in 1894. For two years Henderson prospected in the moose pasture and found promising gravel on a creek he called Gold Bottom. In July 1896 he saw Carmack and told him of the discovery.

As a result Carmack and his brothers-in-law, Skookum Jim and Tagish Charlie, ascended the Tron-Deg about a mile then turned up a tributary, Rabbit Creek. They fought their way through the brush to Gold Bottom but didn't stake; instead they decided to explore further on Rabbit Creek. As they left, Henderson asked Carmack to let him know if he found anything of value on Rabbit Creek.

On the way downstream progress was slow since they were out of provisions and Skookum Jim was hunting for meat. He shot a moose, and while waiting for the others went to Rabbit Creek for a drink. To his surprise he noticed that the sand was flecked with gold. On August 17 the trio staked claims on Rabbit, a name soon changed to the more appropriate "Bonanza." The river it joined, the Tron-Deg, also acquired a new name—the Klondike.

On his way to Fortymile to record the claims, Carmack told everyone he met about the discovery. As a consequence, virtually all miners then in the district staked claims that made them rich. One of the few who didn't stake was Henderson. Carmack never informed him of the strike.

So isolated was the Yukon, however, that the outside world was almost a year learning of the bonanza. By then a new community called Dawson City was being hammered together amidst brush and swamp at the junction of the Tron-Deg and Yukon Rivers. Here veteran trader Joe Ladue, after learning of Carmack's discovery, decided to stake 160

The upper photo is Fortymile in 1896 when it was the largest settlement in the Yukon. The photo above shows the sternwheeler Daisy Bell *on the Athabasca River in 1898, bound for the Klondike.*

acres of land instead of a claim on the creeks. His choice proved favorable since lots eventually sold for $20,000 and more.

The first building at Dawson City was Ladue's log cabin, which doubled as a saloon. By June 1897 the population was already 600, but within a year would soar to 30 or more times this figure for the world was about to learn of the August 17 strike. At the waterfront lay two sternwheelers, the *Alice* and the *Portus B. Weare*. Struggling aboard were miners with gold in blankets, cans, jars, boxes and bags. When the *Alice* left Dawson she carried 25 miners from the creeks of the moose pasture, some $500,000 in gold with them. The *Portus B. Weare* took aboard 60 men with nearly $1 million. At St. Michael the newly rich passengers transferred to two ocean-going steamers, the *Excelsior* and the *Portland*.

Exelsior arrived at San Francisco on July 15, 1897. Within hours glowing accounts of her treasure spread across the continent. When the *Portland* arrived in Seattle two days

later 5,000 people greeted her; then when a local newspaper recorded that she carried "a ton of gold," the biggest gold rush in history erupted.

Every vessel that could float was quickly jammed far beyond capacity. The returning *Excelsior* turned away 10 men for each one that boarded. The *Amur* had normal accommodation for 60 cabin and 100 steerage passengers. Somehow she hauled over 500 passengers and at least as many dogs. The *Willamette* squeezed aboard 1,100 passengers and 300 horses, even though she didn't have chairs to seat one-third that many people, let alone feed them. An awning stretched over part of the deck sheltered about 300 men but, as a passenger later wrote: ". . . about 700 or 800 are compelled to stand or sit out in the rain . . . or go below and stand where the smell is sickening."

Among vessels resurrected to participate in the passenger bonanza was the paddlewheeler *Eliza Anderson*. A 39-year-old veteran of the 1858 Fraser River gold rush, she was now a roadhouse-gambling hall near Seattle. Never-

This photo, taken at midnight in Dawson City on June 28, 1898, shows the arrival of the sternwheeler Seattle No. 1. Aboard were disgruntled gold seekers who had booked passage the year before with W. D. Wood, who was mayor of Seattle when the world learned of the rich strike on the Klondike. Wood promptly resigned and formed a company to provide "through" transportation to the gold-laden creeks.

When passengers reached St. Michael they discovered that there was no river boat to continue the journey and had to help build one. The result was the Seattle No. 1, nicknamed the "Mukluk" since she resembled that piece of Eskimo footwear. Along with many other vessels she was caught by winter on the Yukon and didn't reach Dawson City until June. By then, passengers had been on the way for 314 days.

theless she was pulled from the mud and outfitted for the hazardous voyage northward. The first phase would take the aging vessel 900 miles up the B.C.-Alaska coast then across the open North Pacific Ocean to Kodiak. Then would come another 650 miles to Unalaska in the storm- and fog-swept Aleutian Islands, followed by 800 miles of grey Bering Sea to St. Michael.

Since the *Eliza Anderson* had too deep a draft to cross the Yukon delta, her promoters thoughtfully included a sternwheeler for the upstream journey. She was the *W. K. Merwin,* formerly used to carry farm produce on the Skagit River. The sternwheeler, along with a private yacht and a coal-laden hulk to refuel the *Eliza Anderson,* would be towed by the tug *Richard Holyoke.* All passengers — including 16 squeezed aboard the *W. K. Merwin* — should be gleaning "nuggets like walnuts" within two months.

The *Eliza Anderson* left Seattle August 10, her accommodation so oversold that only the appearance of Captain Tom Powers prevented enraged passengers tossing the unfortunate purser overboard. At that he probably would have been safer than continuing for, among other things, the vessel didn't even have a ship's compass. One passenger, Thomas Wiedemann, later wrote a book about his experiences, *Cheechako into Sourdough,* and described the voyage as "a series of disasters."

At her first stop, Comox, on Vancouver Island, the *Eliza Anderson* rammed a sailing vessel, damaging her paddlewheel box and galley. At Kodiak her deck crew decided that it was easier to hide sacks than fill them with coal. Consequently, she ran out of fuel fighting a vicious North Pacific gale. Her coal bunkers were chopped up and burned, followed by her water tanks, furniture and stateroom partitions. By now she was wallowing like a monstrous box, kept afloat only by her wheezing water pumps. Then they clogged.

"Grab anything that will float," the mate instructed— optimistic advice since anything wooden was rapidly going into the firebox or had washed overboard, including all four liferafts and all but one lifeboat. Then an incredible circumstance saved the 116 on board from imminent death.

A local fisherman named Erik Heestad had stowed away at Kodiak. When he realized the vessel was foundering he left his hiding place and strode to the wheelhouse. He took over the helm, swung the vessel around and headed for the rocky shore of Kodiak Island. Here he brought her to a sheltered cove, the site of an abandoned salmon cannery that included 75 tons of unused coal. With this fuel the battered vessel reached Unalaska but was heavily damaged when she thumped into the wharf. Her disgruntled passengers promptly abandoned her, some returning to Seattle, others continuing across the Bering Sea in a sealing schooner to St. Michael.

Here they found the *W. K. Merwin* ready to proceed upstream. They gratefully boarded her and on October 10 headed upstream. But their journey was short since winter caught them in the tundra country — still 1,400 miles from the "nuggets like walnuts." Nine months and one day later they resumed their journey, finally arriving at Dawson City in August 1898. Instead of taking under two months, the voyage lasted a few days short of one year.

The *Eliza Anderson,* meanwhile, had blown ashore. "The

Eliza Anderson at last a total wreck," states a news item in the *Seattle Post-Intelligencer,* almost in relief. "The wreck in the far north is a fitting end to the old steamer which has several times been rescued from the boneyard . . . ."

The near-fatal adventures of the 116 men on the *Eliza Anderson* were experienced by tens of thousands of other gold seekers. For instance, from Edmonton were two routes. One was 1,500 miles through the rugged wilderness of Alberta, B.C. and Yukon. Of 800 who challenged this route, 160 reached the Yukon, many after a year of struggle, while at least 35 died on the way. The second route from Edmonton was down the Mackenzie River almost to the Arctic Ocean then westward over the Rocky Mountain divide to the Yukon watershed. Nearly 1,700 men and one sternwheeler took this route. About 700 men and the sternwheeler succeeded.

She was the *Daisy Bell,* a home-made craft with an 8-hp engine from the North Saskatchewan River. Her only real problem was the divide between the Mackenzie-Yukon wa-

One of the main portals to Yukon was Skagway, shown above in 1898. The wharf at the right was built by Captain William Moore of Lower Fraser and Stikine River fame. In 1887, 10 years before the Klondike stampede, he pre-empted 160 acres on the flats. As he and his son, Ben, chopped the first tree to start construction of a house and a wharf, the adventurous Captain remarked: "I fully expect before many years to see a pack trail through this pass, followed by a wagon road, and I would not be at all surprised to see a railroad through to the lakes." Just over a decade later, his prophecy became fact.

The pass to which the Captain referred was the White Pass which he discovered in 1887 while packing supplies into the Yukon for surveyor W. Ogilvie. In 1896 Captain Moore undertook two more trips into the Yukon to deliver mail for the Canadian government through 700 miles of virtually uninhabited wilderness to Fortymile. He completed his last trip by dog team in the middle of Yukon winter with temperatures 50 below and colder. About a week before the Captain left Fortymile, three young men preceded him, leaving the community with a "flourish of banners and blare of trumpets," their intention to set a record for speed. Captain Moore not only overtook them on the trail but probably saved their lives since their outfit had broken down, they were almost out of provisions and very dispirited. The venerable Captain was then 73.

tersheds. Here she had to be hauled across by man-power and 30 dogs. As J. G. MacGregor summarized in his book *The Klondike Rush Through Edmonton:* "The *Daisy Bell* . . . made one of the most remarkable trips on record and was the only steamer to cross the mountains into the Yukon."

The most deadly route was that chosen by three parties who attempted to reach the Yukon across Canada's highest mountains, the glacier-covered St. Elias range. Of 100 men who set out, 41 died. One party of 18 had four survivors; two of them with permanently impaired vision, the other two blind.

Main portals to Klondike, however, were two passes, Chilkoot and White, that led from the head of Lynn Canal through the Coast Mountains to the headwaters of the Yukon River. Both were horrors, summarized by one weary traveller who commented that "no matter which you take, you'll wish you'd taken the other."

The White Pass was the lowest but was about 45 miles to the Yukon's navigable headwaters compared with 35 miles for the Chilkoot. The White Pass could be used by horses and mules and in their frenzy normally sane men worked and starved to death 3,000 of them. Fortunately for the animals, the Chilkoot Pass was so steep at its summit that only a man could fight his way up. During the winter of 1897-98 over 20,000 men labored up its forbidding incline, each struggling up to three months to move his mandatory ton of supplies and equipment.

At the summit itself conditions were atrocious. The nearest supply of wood was 7 miles away, but this was better than at White Pass since there it was 12 miles. Blizzards on both passes lasted 10 days or more at a time. Colonel S. B. Steele of the N.W.M.P. noted that on March 3 a storm began at Chilkoot Pass and lasted until May 1. In one day 6 feet of snow fell, on another an avalanche buried the trail and killed over 60 men.

The assault on the passes began in late 1897 when the vanguard of men trudged ashore on the mud flats at the

By the spring of 1898 thousands of men were camped along the shores of Lindeman and Bennett Lakes and the banks of the Upper Yukon River. Here they built over 7,000 boats for the final 560 miles of their journey to the creeks of Klondike. As the inexperienced gold seekers hammered whipsawn green lumber into cumbersome craft, the N.W.M.P. circulated among them. "Build the boats long, boys, and build them strong," they advised. "The Yukon is both." On the opposite page, the Prospector woods up along the Stewart River, a major tributary of the Yukon.

head of Lynn Canal. Soon there were 10,000, then 20,000, then 30,000 strung through the Coast Mountains to the headwaters of the Yukon. But even as they desperately battled the awesome obstacles barring their way, many already in Dawson City were as desperately trying to leave.

Their problem was caused by low water in the Yukon, especially a section between Circle and Fort Yukon known as Yukon Flats. Here for some 200 miles the channel widens to form a massive 2,000-square-mile maze of shallows, shifting sandbars and blind channels. Because "it is impossible to get a three-foot steamer over a twenty-two-inch bar," sternwheelers bringing in Dawson's winter food supply were unable to thread through Yukon Flats.

But unexpectedly the river rose. The *Portus B. Weare* and the *Bella,* by leaving part of the cargo, bumped their way over the sandbars to Circle. Here they encountered an equally formidable obstacle. The trading companies, in an attempt to supply Dawson, had ignored the needs of the miners at Circle.

But these men were veterans. They knew that gold, however valuable, did nothing to stop the rumblings of an empty stomach — especially when the nearest food was 1,500 miles away. They checked supplies in the two stores at Circle, and balanced the results with what each miner required. Then they appointed a committee to demand that the difference be taken off the next sternwheeler. The *Portus B. Weare* was consequently greeted by determined men with loaded rifles. Twenty tons of supplies remained behind, a further 37 tons when the *Bella* arrived. Then the miners paid for and received their winter outfits in the normal manner.

The *Bella* reached Dawson on September 30. The same day a chilling notice was posted by Inspector C. Constantine of the N.W.M.P. It read, in part: "For those who have not laid in a winter's supply to remain here longer is to court death from starvation, or at least a certainty of sickness from scurvy and other troubles. Starvation now stares everyone in the face who is hoping for outside relief . . . ."

Ice was the greatest hazard to navigation on the Yukon River. The river could—and did—freeze solid overnight, trapping vessels and frequently destroying them next spring at break-up. Drift ice was an additional hazard. It quickly rasped through the hull of a sternwheeler not protected by iron plates. The upper photo shows the Whitehorse in early October; the lower one, Seattle No. 3 after she was pitched ashore by ice at Rampart.

On the opposite page men bound for Klondike hurriedly check for mail at Tagish in early 1898. As yet they didn't realize that of the ton of equipment and supplies that each struggled with, the least useful items would be their rifle and goldpan.

Scores of those without winter outfits left on scows and various small craft. To encourage others the Canadian Government offered free passage on the *Bella* plus five days' food. She left for Fort Yukon and other downstream points on October 21, passengers cramming her decks, messroom and even perching on the cordwood. Among them were some of the 1,800 men who had bought through passage from Seattle and other points when the arrival of the *Portland* with its "ton of gold" startled the world. ". . . exactly 43 reached Dawson," reported Edwin Adney, a correspondent for *Harper's Weekly* and *The London Chronicle* who who was in Dawson at the time, "and of these upwards of 35, having no outfits, were compelled to return on the *Bella* and *Weare*. The rest of the unfortunates . . . were scattered at various points along the Yukon."

Joining the stranded were those on board the two sternwheelers. At Circle their captains decided that ice was too dangerous to proceed further. In all, some 2,500 men plus a sprinkling of women spent nine months isolated along 1,400 miles of the Yukon.

While they passed the frigid, sunless days on board stranded sternwheelers, the barges they towed, or rough shelters on shore, the army assailing White and Chilkoot Passes slogged forward. When the days lengthened and weather warmed, over 30,000 were camped along a 50-mile section of the river's headwaters, most of them on two lakes, Lindeman and Bennett. Here they hammered together a weird assembly of over 7,000 boats to carry them 560 miles down the Upper Yukon to the golden creeks of Klondike.

Included in the homespun armada were sternwheelers, their engines, boilers, and other ironware packed over White and Chilkoot Passes by men, mules, horses and dogs. The vessels were hurriedly assembled on the shore of Lake Bennett and as hurriedly launched. One Klondiker, Julius M. Price, watched a launching at Lake Bennett in June 1898. "Into the water it glided majestically," he wrote, "without attracting more attention than our own departure, which was not much."

On May 29 the ice left Lake Bennett, followed by the greatest flotilla of boats the north has known. At the insistence of the N.W.M.P. each carried a registration number and by June 18 over 7,100 boats carrying 28,000 men with some 30 million pounds of provisions checked past the police post at Tagish. Major hazard was a 3-mile-long section about 100 miles downstream from Lake Bennett. Here the river constricts to form Miles Canyon, a 100-foot-wide slot flanked by sheer basalt rock walls, and Whitehorse Rapids, a turbulence of white water where a hastily dug grave became the end of the trail for scores of Klondikers. But in 1898 those who wished could avoid the 3-mile-long turmoil by having their goods hauled over a wooden-railed tramway that paralleled the bank. At the lower end of the tramway grew a community called Whitehorse, one day to become the largest city in the Yukon.

The first sternwheeler to challenge Miles Canyon was the *Bellingham*. She left Lake Bennett on June 5, quickly followed by eight more. She successfully shot Miles Canyon and Whitehorse Rapids, although one of those following, the *Joseph Clossett*, bounced off the basalt columns a couple of times and sank at the head of the Rapids. She was later put back in service and operated between Dawson City and Whitehorse, which became the head of navigation.

The *Bellingham* completed her pioneering voyage on June 14. It was fairly routine, although at one point she went aground. However she was towing a scow laden with six tons of equipment and staff for an about-to-be established bank in Dawson and it kept going, dragging the sternwheeler into deeper water. The scow proved equally independent on another occasion when the pair came to an island in the channel. To the horror of all, the *Bellingham* went down one side, the scow down the other. Fortunately those aboard the scow cast off lines seconds ahead of disaster.

The *Bellingham,* however, wasn't the first sternwheeler to reach Dawson in 1898. That record went to *May West.* She arrived on June 8 after spending the winter frozen in below the Tanana River. Her main cargo was 16 barrels of whiskey which immediately went on sale at $1 a drink.

The first through vessel from St. Michael was the *Monarch* which arrived at 7 p.m., July 21, 1898. The *Klondike Nugget,* one of two newspapers now established in Dawson,

reported: "She is a strongly built boat of goodly proportions with excellent accommodations . . . and was built especially for the Yukon trade this winter at Ballard, Washington. She has made a remarkably successful trip all the way from Seattle. . . ."

After her, sternwheelers arrived so frequently that the staffs of the two newspapers could barely keep record. This activity wasn't surprising since never in the history of northwest rivers had a sternwheeler fleet been so quickly assembled.

In Seattle, the Moran shipyard built 12 "by the mile and cut them off when necessary." The first, the *J. P. Light,* was launched on April 23 with steam up and by May 25 the fleet was completed. Each could carry 400 tons of cargo, with first-class staterooms for 24 passengers and standing room for 200 more. Covered by a $600,000 Lloyd's of London insurance policy they headed northward, challenging the 2,350 miles of North Pacific and Bering Sea under their own steam. Somewhat battered, all except the *Western Star*

arrived safely. She was blown ashore off the Alaska Coast while the fleet sheltered from a gale. The others paid for themselves on their first voyage.

The Canadian Pacific Railway planned a fleet of 20 vessels to ply the Stikine River to Telegraph Creek, first part of an "All-Canadian" route to the goldfields. From Telegraph Creek a 150-mile-long railway was to be built to Teslin Lake where additional sternwheelers would connect to Dawson. The railway plan folded but not until many of the vessels were ready. A number were diverted to the Yukon, adding to the colorful host that plied the river in 1898.

There was the *Dusty Diamond* and the *Gold Star*, the *Ida May* and the *Rock Island*, the *City of Paris* and the *Clifford Sifton*, the *Columbian* and the *Bonanza King*. There was the *J. P. Light*, the *Kilburn*, *Lightning*, *Linda* and *Anglian*, built at Teslin Lake with machinery hauled 150 miles by sleigh over the projected route of the railway from Telegraph Creek.

There was the *Pilgrim*, *Quickstep*, *Sovereign*, *Canadian* and *Philip B. Low*, a vessel which sank so often she became

known as the "*Fill-up Below.*" There was the *Glenora*, *Iowa*, *Louise*, *Tacoma*, *Willie Irving*, and the *Yukoner*—the latter operated for one trip by spirited Captain John Irving of Lower Fraser River fame.

The *Yukoner* was built in Victoria but assembled at St. Michael and launched with champagne by a blonde dance-hall girl. Her maiden voyage maintained this gay atmosphere. Although no one knew how—or where—she crowded aboard 300 passengers, mostly musicians, actors, dance-hall girls and gamblers, plus a generous cargo of liquor. Since Captain Irving disliked routine, the maiden voyage was lively and entertaining. At landings he headed for bank or wharf with throttle wide open, paddlewheel churning white foam and whistle blasting. Then as disaster seemed imminent he would go full astern and glide majestically to a stop. Occasionally he misjudged, but that was part of the fun. On his Yukon voyage he refined this technique by having a band playing and dance-hall girls swirling around the deck. If it was a wooding-up stop, as a final gesture wood choppers

The Sarah and her sisters, Hannah and Susie, were the Yukon's queens during the gold rush. The Casca, Columbian and Monarch, opposite, were built in Victoria and Seattle and, under their own power, made the dangerous ocean voyage north in 1898. That July, the Monarch was the first through sternwheeler to reach Dawson City from St. Michael.

The Nora and her two sisters, the Flora and Ora, were built at Lake Bennett in 1898. Initially they furnished transportation only, with passengers having to provide their own bedding and meals. They did offer running water, although it was basic, consisting of "a zinc bucket which one lowered over the side of the steamer. . . ."

came aboard for champagne.

But of the sternwheelers which plied the Yukon, the queens were the *Sarah*, *Susie* and *Hannah*, owned by the Alaska Commercial Co. Patterned after the famed Ohio River breed the $110,000 vessels were 222-feet long with twin stacks and 1,000 hp engines which drove them 17 miles an hour. Bed linen and blankets were monogrammed with Company initials while the mahogany dining room was complete with silver service. They had comfortable accommodation for 150 passengers but could carry 500 "in the manner of the country," a term which meant that passengers slept in their own blankets wherever they found room.

Unfortunately, the gold rush they were built to serve ended as abruptly as it began. During the summer of 1898 Dawson City exploded into one of the largest cities in Western Canada and U.S. But it was a fleeting development—for it and for the sternwheelers the pall of obscurity was already descending. The majority of the incoming thousands quickly realized that virtually all gravel of value had been staked even before they left on their months-long ordeal. They realized, also, that the closest they would come to "nuggets like walnuts" was in their own imagination. Thousands quietly pushed their boats into the current and continued downstream towards home.

Other thousands sold their outfits for what they could get, and as the summer days lengthened, it wasn't much. Flour that had soared to $120 for a 50-pound sack during Dawson's food crisis the previous October was $3 a sack in June. Rifles that cost $45 each a few months before were $1 each—if bought by the dozen.

In contrast to the food-short months of the winter, Dawson now groaned with supplies. In addition to millions of pounds carried by the stampeders, massive tonnages arrived by sternwheelers. By September, 56 vessels delivered 7,540 tons and another 20 were on the way. Their cargo included plate glass mirrors for bars and hanging oil lamps for dance halls, silks for prostitutes and uniforms for the

Salvation Army, bibles for the churches and 120,000 gallons of liquor for the thirsty.

A rough estimate of Dawson's population was 18,000, although when the main influx arrived there were probably 30,000 or more. But by autumn thousands had left, then word of a new gold strike at Nome on the Bering Sea accelerated the exodus.

Among the first outward bound vessels was the *W. K. Merwin.* She left May 31, 1899, so crowded her passengers stood "like straphangers on a streetcar"; so short of food that those onboard had to shoot waterfowl and gather eggs to augment their cornmeal diet. For the *W. K. Merwin,* the voyage was her last. On August 2 she was destroyed by Nome's powerful breakers.

While the *W. K. Merwin* was ending her career and while Dawson City flared and darkened, profound changes were taking place at the Yukon's headwaters.

In May 1898 construction started on a 110-mile railway, the White Pass and Yukon, to link Skagway with White-

horse. The project was considered impossible by most people except project engineer M. J. "Big Mike" Haney. He never wavered, despite many unusual problems. On August 8, 1898, for instance, 1,300 out of 2,000 employees abruptly left when they learned of a new strike on the east shore of Lake Atlin in northwestern B.C. Many didn't wait for their pay, although they did take virtually every pick and shovel the railway firm owned. But by October ranks were filled again and the last spike pounded at Lake Bennett on July 29, 1900. Vancouver and Seattle were now only 8 days from Dawson City, the numbing Chilkoot Pass already history.

Next year the White Pass expanded its transportation services. It bought the John Irving Navigation Company which served the Atlin-Bennett Lake region and the Canadian Development Company which operated a winter stage line from Whitehorse to Dawson. Included were several sternwheelers. To operate them the White Pass formed a river division, British Yukon Navigation Company, or B.Y.N.

Front Street, Dawson City, in 1899. By then the community had reached its zenith and was rapidly waning. Destined to replace it as capital and administrative center of the Yukon was Whitehorse, shown on the opposite page about

1904. The lower photo shows the Tutshi on Tagish Lake, part of the Yukon River's headwaters on the B.C.-Yukon border. Launched in 1917, the Tutshi served until 1953.

as it was soon called. The firm built three new vessels: the 779-ton *Dawson*, 777-ton *Selkirk* and 1,120-ton *Whitehorse*, and bought several others, including the colorful *Yukoner*.

While the White Pass and Yukon was organizing its transportation network, a sternwheeler named *Lavelle Young* was helping found a community that became the second largest city in Alaska. In July 1901 she was hired by a trader named Captain E. T. Barnette to ascend a Yukon tributary, the Tanana, some 400 miles where Barnette intended to trade with the Indians. About 200 miles upstream she "ran out of water" and Barnette had to unload. He was so annoyed that he refused to shake hands with Captain Adams when the *Lavelle Young* churned away—and not without reason. His wife was crying, he faced a bleak cold winter, and he had 125 tons of goods to trade with the Indians but not an Indian within miles. The only apparent customers were two prospectors who appeared out of the bush when they saw smoke from the *Lavelle Young*.

But one of them was Felix Pedro who, one year later, discovered gold on a nearby creek. When the inevitable rush started Barnette changed the name of his trading post to Fairbanks. The creeks eventually yielded $35 million and Barnette grew rich. Fairbanks grew into the largest community in the Yukon watershed and terminus of both the Alaska Railroad and the Alaska Highway.

While the rush was on to Fairbanks, the day of the individual miner was ending on the creeks of Klondike. By 1905 with picks and shovels they had removed some $100 million from the frozen gravel but an equal amount remained. Needed to remove it was capital and machinery. One firm that moved in was the Guggenheims of New York. They acquired control of Eldorado, Bonanza and other creeks and in 1906 started constructing a $3 million, 70-mile-long ditch to bring water for hydraulic mining. Additional millions went to construct a fleet of seven dredges to rip up the gravel.

Sternwheelers continued to be the main means of transportation but scores were now ashore and abandoned. Oth-

The Scotia, at top, on Lake Atlin in northern B.C., was launched in June 1899 and served Atlin residents until 1918. She was beached in front of the town and finally burned in 1967.

The lower photo of the D. A. Thomas leaving the trading post of Fort St. John about 1920 illustrates sternwheel activity on another portion of northern B.C.—the Peace River. Paddlewheel days on this section of river opened in 1903 when the small Catholic Mission sternwheeler St. Charles was launched about 50 miles downstream from the present town of Grande Prairie. The vessel reflected the vitality of Bishop Grouard, probably the best known of all the northern priests and one of Canada's great frontiersmen. For nearly 70 years from 1862 he served the Indians and Eskimoes, travelling tens of thousands of miles by foot and snowshoe, dogteam and canoe. His travels took him past the site of future Dawson City to the Bering Sea decades before the Klondike rush. When settlers started moving into the magnificent Peace River country in 1907 he had already served the region over 40 years.

His small sternwheeler operated 525 miles upstream from rapids called Vermilion Shutes to Hudson's Hope, a few miles below the Peace River Canyon, carrying supplies for the mission at Fort St. John plus goods for the N.W.M.P. and the H.B.C. In 1905 the latter firm added its own vessel to the river. She was the Peace River, 110 feet long with a

capacity of 40 tons. She served until 1915, then next year appeared the D. A. Thomas.

This sternwheeler, largest to serve on the Peace River, could carry 250 tons of freight and 140 passengers. She was built at a cost of $119,000 for Welsh coal millionaire, Lord Rhondda. He intended to develop an immense coal field at Hudson's Hope and also hoped to discover oil in the Peace River country. So confident was he of success that he had oil tanks fitted to the D. A. Thomas, but because of the First World War he discontinued his project after spending $250,000 in surveys and explorations. Had he not been interrupted he could well have discovered the immense oil and gas deposits uncovered in the Peace River country after World War Two.

The D. A. Thomas was laid up in 1922, then in 1924 acquired by the H.B.C. However the 167-foot vessel proved too large for the Peace River and in 1931 was taken through Vermilion Shutes to the lower part of the Peace.

The last sternwheeler to ply the Upper Peace was the Alcan, a small sternwheeler built during World War Two to aid construction of the Alaska Highway suspension bridge over the Peace River.

The photo on the opposite page shows the Dawson about to enter Five Finger rapids between Whitehorse and Dawson City. The Dawson plied the river for a quarter of a century, from 1901 to 1926.

ers died more tragically.

On September 25, 1906, the *Columbian* was bound for Dawson on her last trip of the season. A crew member decided to shoot some ducks, but unfortunately stumbled and fired into three tons of blasting powder on the bow. A furnace of flame enveloped the bow while the blast shattered the wheelhouse glass, blew Captain Williams off his feet and severed engine-room controls. The Captain slid down a rope to the guard rail and made his way to the engine room. "For God's sake, Frank, stand by the engines or we are all doomed," he yelled to chief engineer Frank Mavis.

Just then one of the victims, completely on fire, staggered into the engine room. "I pulled what little clothes he had left on," Mavis later wrote to his wife, "and covered him with cylinder oil. By this time the engine room was full of smoke and fire was breaking through the bulkhead. The man lying at my feet making the most dreadful shrieking I ever heard and me standing at the throttle unable to give him any assistance."

The burning vessel was finally made fast ashore and the dead and dying laid on the beach. Then Captain Williams, Frank Mavis and second mate Smith undertook a 60-mile round trip by raft and canoe to summon aid. Of the seven men standing closest to the powder kegs only one survived. He was a stowaway.

Because of steadily dwindling traffic, the *Columbian* wasn't replaced for 5 years. Then in 1911 the B.Y.N. launched the *Casca,* a 1,079-ton sternwheeler which became their flagship. Next they added the *Nasutlin,* and in 1913, the *Yukon.*

By now the B.Y.N. was engaged in a rate war with Northern Navigation, the major U.S. firm still on the river. Fares between Whitehorse and Dawson dropped from $26 to $5, a rate that officials of both companies knew would bankrupt them. Consequently, they "reached an agreement." In April 1914, the White Pass bought Northern Navigation.

But in 1923 came new competition for the B.Y.N.—and to it there was no answer. A railway was completed from Seward on Alaska's southern coast 460 miles to Fairbanks. Additional sternwheelers joined the scores already decaying

along the river and at St. Michael, where Bill MacBride once counted over 50 falling apart, including the majestic *Sarah*, *Susie* and *Hannah*. The B.Y.N. operated 11 vessels on the Canadian section of the river but these gradually dwindled.

The *Dawson* was wrecked in Rink Rapids in 1926, the *Selkirk* in the fall of 1930. In 1936 the Thirty Mile River claimed both the *Klondike* and the *Casca*.

Then in 1937 there was a flurry. From the shipyard in Whitehorse came a new 1,363-ton *Klondike* and a 1,300-ton *Casca*. In addition the *Keno* was rebuilt and the *Nasutlin* thoroughly overhauled. However it was the last major sternwheel building project in North America. The White Pass and Yukon Route had now added airplanes to its transportation network, the sternwheelers were becoming part of a bygone era. So, too, it seemed was the Yukon for the population continued dropping. By 1939 there were fewer than 5,000 people in the entire territory.

But that year World War Two erupted. Part of its legacy was a 1,523-mile highway linking Dawson Creek in B.C. through Whitehorse to Fairbanks in Alaska. Stimulated by new roads, the Yukon's population increased, but for the sternwheelers events followed an inevitable pattern. Roads radiated from the Alaska Highway and in 1951 one of them linked the mining community of Mayo to Whitehorse. Ore from the mines now went by truck instead of by riverboat. Three of six paddlewheelers still in service were laid up. Then in 1953 a road was completed to Dawson City. The remaining sternwheelers were hauled onto the ways at Whitehorse, their working days over.

The *Klondike* was given a reprieve when the White Pass and Yukon, in conjunction with Canadian Pacific Airlines, spent $100,000 refurbishing her to stimulate summer tourist trade. She was fitted with dance floor, lounge, full bar, and even a $1,000 record player. But the experiment wasn't successful. In 1955 she, too, was hauled ashore at Whitehorse for the last time. Among vessels beside her on the bank was the *Yukoner*, the one on which Captain Irving made his unconventional upstream voyage 57 years before.

But in 1957 the *Yukoner* was sold for firewood. It appear-

During the gold rush the Olive May, upper left, was frozen in at the head of Lake Laberge. Shortly afterward the N.W.M.P. post at Tagish learned that a miner who lived in a cabin near the vessel was sick with scurvy. A doctor named Sugden was sent to help but found the man dead. Since Dr. Sugden was unable to dig a grave because of the frozen ground, he solved the burial problem by cremating the unfortunate miner in the firebox of the Olive May. Later Dr. Sugden became friends with a bank clerk in Whitehorse and told him of the incident. The clerk wove the cremation, the sternwheeler and the miner into a robust poem, The Cremation of Sam McGee. In 1907 this and other of the clerk's poems appeared in a booklet which sold over 1 million copies. The clerk-poet, Robert W. Service, became famous and wealthy. Dr. Sugden wasn't so fortunate. In 1926 while waving goodbye to friends at Mayo he fell off a barge being towed by the Canadian, center, and drowned. The Keno, opposite, squeezes under the Carmacks bridge on her way to Dawson City in 1960. She is now preserved as a museum at the former capital of the Yukon.

The Yukoner, star of Captain Irving's gala upstream voyage. Legend persists that the subsequent party in Dawson City cost some $30,000. The Klondike, at top, closed Yukon sternwheel days in 1955. She is today a National Historic Site at Whitehorse. Another veteran, the Keno, is preserved at Dawson City. She and the Whitehorse are shown on the following pages. The photo of the Whitehorse was taken about 1901 in 80-foot wide Five Finger Rapids. She logged over 1 million miles during her career and won the nickname "Old Gray Mare." On page 156 is a menu from her dining saloon.

ed that the rest would join her, including the *Tutshi* which after a long career on Tagish Lake had been hauled ashore at Carcross near the end of Bennett Lake. Then the White Pass and Yukon Route gave the *Whitehorse, Casca, Klondike* and *Keno* to the Canadian Government for preservation as National Historic Sites.

As a result, the *Keno* became the last sternwheeler to ply the Yukon River. On August 26, 1960, under command of Captain F. S. Blakely, a veteran sternwheel skipper from B.C.'s Columbia River, with Frank Slim, a Stikine River Indian, as pilot, she left for Dawson City to become a museum. On August 29 she arrived safely and, despite pouring rain, was greeted by virtually the entire population, which had dwindled to under 500.

She has been preserved and restored, as has the *Klondike* at Whitehorse. Both vessels are now National Historic Sites and open to the public. The *Whitehorse, Casca* and *Tutshi* weren't so fortunate.

The Federal Government wasn't too enthusiastic with its gift of the *Whitehorse* and the *Casca* and announced that it wanted to get rid of them "one way or the other." Tenders were called for their destruction but Whitehorse residents vigorously objected. In a dramatic reprieve tenders were withdrawn only hours before they were to be opened. Unfortunately, the reprieve was temporary. The vessels continued to be neglected and on June 20, 1974, both were destroyed in a fire probably started by transients.

The *Tutshi* was similarly ill-fated. For nearly 20 years she lay a derelict at Carcross. Then in 1971 the Yukon government bought her for restoration. but progress was slow. Finally, after 17 years and $1 million, she was opened to the public. Her new career was tragically brief. On July 25, 1990, the *Tutshi* was destroyed by a fire that many believe was arson.

Today the *Klondike* and the *Keno* are the only survivors of some 250 sternwheelers which once plied the over 2000-mile-long Yukon River and other northern waters.

S. S. WHITEHORSE

C. M. COGHLAN
Master

"The table's spread. come, let us dine, my friend"

DINNER

Prohibition Cocktail

Yukon Radishes   Green Onions   Leaf Lettuce

Dawson City Tomatoes   Queen Olives

SOUPS
Consomme Clear   Cream of Oyster

FISH
Baked Marsh Lake Whitefish, Sauce au Dam

ENTREES
Boiled Brisket of Pelly River Beef, Sauce Tantalus

Macaroni au Grautin   Pineapple Fritters

ROASTS
Stuffed Haunch of Carmacks Veal
Roast Loin of Stewart River Moose with Jelly

VEGETABLES
Mashed Moosehide Potatoes   Mazie May Garden Peas

Sunnydale Spinach

DESSERT
Bonanza Plum Pudding, Hard Rock Sauce

Sourdough Blueberry Pie   Cheechaco Apple Pie

Assorted '98 Cakes   Golden Fruit

Nuggets of Cheese   Christie's Crackers

Hudsons Bay Tea   Five Fingers of Coffee

Index